Whispers of God

Liturgical Resources
for Year B

Lavon Bayler

The Pilgrim Press
NEW YORK

Library of Congress Cataloging-in-Publication Data

Bayler, Lavon, 1933–
   Whispers of God.

   Includes indexes.
   1. Worship programs.   I. Title.
   BV198.B33   1987   264'.13   87-23596
   ISBN 0-8298-0758-6

The Pilgrim Press, 132 West 31 Street, New York, NY 10001

With unending thanks
to
Bob Bayler
partner in marriage and ministry
home and family
for thirty great years

Contents

Introduction

When have you heard the whispers of God? When the tiny fingers of a newborn child curled around your own? When dancing flames of a campfire illuminated the faces of newfound friends with whom you had played and worked and worshiped? When the first crocus of spring emerged through newfallen snow? When you were reconciled with one whom you had fought? When the struggles of an ancient psalmist mirrored your own? At the bedside of a loved one who slipped into eternity with a smile?

Day by day as I encountered passages from the lectionary to wrest from them the words and phrases through which people might join in the work of worship, I was aware of the "still small voice" that Elijah had discerned after the fire and whirlwind and storm. "Have you heard the whispers of God?" I asked one Sunday morning in a sermon to a responsive congregation. Now you have in your hands my efforts to respond to the Spirit's leading as this book grew into a resource for personal devotion and corporate worship.

Whispers of God: Liturgical Resources for Year B (unlike *Fresh Winds of the Spirit*, its predecessor based on the lectionary for Year A) follows a standard format. For each occasion in the church year, I have written a hymn, responsive call to worship, invocation, call to confession, prayer of confession, assurance of forgiveness, collect, offertory invitation, offertory prayer, and responsive commission and blessing. All are inspired by the suggested scriptures and use many words and phrases from the texts. As a worship leader, you can choose those elements you need for a particular service, adapting them to your special requirements and emphases. Selections may be copied in worship bulletins; the required acknowledgment appears on the copyright page.

Congregational participation in the liturgy is sought whenever possible. However, the sections designed for responsive reading could be presented by two persons reading alternately. Often the leader's portion of the call to worship or commission and blessing can stand alone or be easily adapted for use without congregational response.

In some seasons the scriptures for up to six weeks have been considered together to form some common worship elements that are used week after week. The reinforcement of repeated usage has real merit and power. Indeed, within each occasion's resources the repetition of words and phrases from the day's Bible readings is meant to awaken worshipers to the meaning of the words.

Preparation for worship is appropriate not only for leaders, but also for members of the congregation. Small groups reflecting together on the lectionary readings for an upcoming Sunday might also use these worship resources to enliven their approach to corporate worship. Perhaps participants would spark one another's creativity so that additional resources are made available to pastors as they shape each worship event.

Thanks again to the painstaking thoroughness of my son David Bayler, you have available an index to follow key words and phrases through the entire book if you are planning worship thematically, instead of beginning with the lectionary. The topical index of hymns will point you to new lyrics that may be useful in worship settings other than the one for which they were designed.

Colleagues in ministry have been helpful with their comments and criticisms as sections were completed and shared for their scrutiny. At the risk of omitting some, I cite, with gratitude, Pat Anderson, Betsy Bacon, "Chris" Christofersen, Jim Christopher, Nan Conser, Zan Harper, Lynda Vacker, and Jim Werner. Very special thanks are due to Pat Kitner, who transformed my handwritten notes into pages of manuscript in the cracks of time between her work as administrative assistant at the Congregational United Church of Christ in St. Charles, Illinois, service on the Northern Association Council, as secretary for the Church and Ministry Committee, and as coordinator for LAMP, our new lay ministry training program, to say nothing of preaching in dozens of churches and all her other interests, projects, and family concerns. Numerous unnamed colleagues have encouraged me and buttressed the empowerment by Word and Spirit that my before-dawn writing times provided in the midst of the busiest year of my life.

More than anything else, I must give credit to the support received from home. Had my husband and three sons been helpless before the stove and washing machine, these words would never have been written. Thanks to Bob, Dave, Jay, and Tim; your enthusiasm for *Fresh Winds of the Spirit* kept me listening for *Whispers of God*.

Liturgical Resources for Year B

The Advent Season

First Sunday of Advent

Old Testament: Isaiah 63:16—64:8
Psalm 80:1–7
Epistle: 1 Corinthians 1:3–9
Gospel: Mark 13:32–37

CALL TO WORSHIP

Come, believers and scoffers, faithful and faithless;
God welcomes us all to this time apart.
We sense God's call, even when we do not reply;
God hears us, even when we do not speak.
Amid prosperity and calamity, God is present,
whether or not we respond.
How shall we know God's salvation if we reject it,
or be healed if we turn away?
Now is the time to await Christ's appearing
and to seek the Spirit's gifts.
We come expectantly, yet fearfully,
knowing that worship may change us.
Amen.   **Amen.**

INVOCATION

The nations tremble before you, Mighty God. Face us with enough of you
in this hour that we, too, may be filled with awe and wonder. Melt our
hard hearts to make space for your love as it comes to us in Jesus Christ.
Amen.

CALL TO CONFESSION

In this Advent Season we are summoned to prepare for God's coming to
us in a form we can begin to understand. Jesus accepted all our human
limitations yet remained faithful to the Eternal law of love. We who have
taken this saving action for granted are called to repent and be watchful.
Let us confess our disobedience.

PRAYER OF CONFESSION

Awesome and Powerful God, we have wandered far from you. You have
trusted us, but we have mistrusted you. We have acted as if you never
called our names or blessed us. No wonder we feel alone before a host of
enemies! Are you angry with us, God? Is there a place for us in your
plans, in spite of our iniquities? We want to take hold of your goodness
and find a new direction for our lives. Save us from ourselves, O God!
Amen.

ASSURANCE OF FORGIVENESS

God is our Parent and our Redeemer, the source of all our unused spiritual gifts. We have been given everything we need for a new life in Christ. Grace and peace come to us now, to equip us for the tasks to which we are called. Receive God's forgiveness with joy, and the assurance of strength to do what God expects. Amen.

COLLECT

Creator of All, who fashions us as a potter works with clay, open us to your good news and help us to respond. Minister to us amid our tears and our weariness, that we may accept your grace and use the gifts we receive from your hand. Ready us for the coming of our Savior. Amen.

OFFERTORY INVITATION

By amazing grace we have received the gifts we are about to share. All that we give—and all that we retain for our own use—is claimed by God. May we bring our offerings and ourselves to proclaim the good news of Advent for our own day.

OFFERTORY PRAYER

We rejoice, O God, in the gifts of your Spirit that offer us productive and fulfilling lives. As we exercise our generosity, touch us with new awareness of sisters and brothers you call us to love. May our gifts and prayers lift them and us into true partnership in your service. Amen.

COMMISSION AND BLESSING

Go forth as faithful believers
who extend God's welcome to a waiting world.
   We will listen for God's messages
   and share the truth we are able to hear.
As God has met you here with healing power,
let your words and deeds extend wholeness to others.
   We will try to see the world through others' eyes
   and respond to their hurts with care.
Grace to you and peace from God, our Mother and Father,
and from the Sovereign Jesus Christ.
   God is faithful
   and will supply everything we need.
Amen.   **Amen.**

(See hymn No. 1.)

Second Sunday of Advent

Old Testament: Isaiah 40:1–11
Psalm 85:8–13
Epistle: 2 Peter 3:8–15a
Gospel: Mark 1:1–8

CALL TO WORSHIP

The God of Peace meets us in this peaceful place,
offering pardon and comfort to those in distress.
We are hurting people, wounded and vulnerable,
in need of forgiveness and reassurance.
Come to this place where valleys are lifted up
and mountains and hills are made low.
We long for some evenness and stability
amid the upheavals of our lives.
God brings salvation to the world's suffering ones
and calls us to be bearers of good news.
We who are not worthy to untie Christ's sandals
accept the challenge to prepare the way for this Advent.

INVOCATION

O God, as your salvation draws near we long for wholeness while clinging
to our brokenness. Speak to us the word we need for our healing. Send
your Spirit to dwell with us and empower our service in both familiar and
unexpected places. In Jesus' name. Amen.

CALL TO CONFESSION

Again, in this Advent Season we are summoned to prepare for God's
coming to us in a form we can begin to understand. Jesus accepted all our
human limitations yet remained faithful to the Eternal law of love. We
who have taken this saving action for granted are called to repent and be
watchful. Let us confess our disobedience.

PRAYER OF CONFESSION

Caring God, who wills that none of us should perish, we confess our
unreadiness for your rule in our midst. We live fragmented lives with no
center of value. Greed, ambition, and desire for safety battle within us.
We become content with withered grass and fading flowers and neglect
your Word, which is forever. Bring a new day to disturb and remake us,
that we may be ready to accept your forgiveness. Amen.

ASSURANCE OF FORGIVENESS

Behold your God! Your salvation is at hand. Accept God's forgiveness and receive the baptism of the Holy Spirit. God will give you all good things you need. Amen.

COLLECT

Prepare us, O God, to hear your Word, which is forever, as we welcome the Christchild. Ready us to receive salvation and to rejoice in the freedom to give ourselves in service. Equip us for the new heaven and new earth in which we may dwell in holiness and godliness. In Jesus' name. Amen.

OFFERTORY INVITATION

By amazing grace we have received the gifts we are about to share. All that we give—and all that we retain for our own use—is claimed by God. May we bring our offerings and ourselves to proclaim the good news of Advent for our own day.

OFFERTORY PRAYER

The land has yielded its increase, and we have been blessed, O God. For all your good gifts we give humble thanks. Now we would share some of your bounty; use these gifts to feed your flocks and carry your lambs to safety. Amen.

COMMISSION AND BLESSING

The God of Peace grant you peace to face a warring world
and courage to be a peacemaker.
**We want to extend the forgiveness we have known
to wounded and hurting people, near and far.**
Lift your voices on the mountains and in the valleys;
witness to truth in all holiness and godliness.
**We seek the excitement of risk-taking for Christ
among those who need what we can give.**
We have been together in the saving presence of God.
Now God goes with us, granting wholeness for all of life.
**In thankfulness and anticipation, we face another week,
with its opportunities and responsibilities.**
Amen.   **Amen.**

(See hymn No. 2.)

Third Sunday of Advent

Old Testament: Isaiah 61:1–4, 8–11
Canticle: Luke 1:46b–55
Epistle: 1 Thessalonians 5:16–24
Gospel: John 1:6–8, 19–28

CALL TO WORSHIP
A voice cries in the wilderness,
and we find ourselves drawn to the message.
God invades the commonplace,
and we cannot evade the changes God brings.
On every hand our values are challenged
as attention is drawn to the lowly and weak.
We are not worthy to untie the sandals
of the Humble Servant, who loved all people.
Draw near to join those who rejoice
in a God who comforts and confronts.
We come to proclaim the worth of God,
and to claim the worth God invests in us.

12/16/90

INVOCATION
Bring us the good news we need, O God of All Holiness, for our spirits
are faint within us. In our weariness we seek comfort, salvation, and
liberation, for ourselves and for all your children. Be among us, revealing
again more than we are ready to hear or see. Attune us to that which we
avoid, and help us to view aright your saving activity. In Jesus' name.
Amen.

CALL TO CONFESSION
Again, in this Advent Season we are summoned to prepare for God's
coming to us in a form we can begin to understand. Jesus accepted all our
human limitations yet remained faithful to the Eternal law of love. We
who have taken this saving action for granted are called to repent and be
watchful. Let us confess our disobedience.

PRAYER OF CONFESSION
Grant us the courage, O God, to admit to you that which we try to hide
from ourselves. You have made us rich and we use your goodness as an
excuse for false pride. You have built up and we have torn down. You have
created and we have destroyed. We call on you for mercy, here and now.
Remove the distortions from our vision and the lethargy from our service.
In Jesus' name. Amen.

ASSURANCE OF FORGIVENESS

God clothes us with salvation and covers us with righteousness. Our sins are forgiven, and we begin anew with opportunities to proclaim God's favor, live our thankfulness, and rejoice in the transforming power of the Holy Spirit. Praise God's holy name today and always! Amen.

COLLECT

Gracious God, who anointed and baptized One to be the Guide for all humanity, unbind us that we may respond to your word and be filled with your Spirit. Equip us to abstain from evil and hold fast to the good, that your will may be advanced through us. Amen.

OFFERTORY INVITATION

By amazing grace we have received the gifts we are about to share. All that we give—and all that we retain for our own use—is claimed by God. May we bring our offerings and ourselves to proclaim the good news of Advent for our own day.

OFFERTORY PRAYER

May our gifts be as generous as your provision for us, O God. Use them to bear witness to the light you sent in Christ Jesus. Move us and all people to prayer, rejoicing, and thanksgiving. As we administer these offerings for their best possible return, keep us faithful to your purposes. Amen.

COMMISSION AND BLESSING

Go out into the world, and God will give you voice.
Proclaim God's good news in word and deed.
Because God has changed us inside,
we are not afraid of changes around us.
Comfort the dispirited and those who mourn.
Abstain from evil; hold fast to what is good.
In the face of injustice, robbery, and wrong,
we would build up rather than destroy.
The God of peace sanctify you wholly
and keep you blameless in body and spirit.
We celebrate the faithfulness of God
and praise God's holy name.
Amen.   **Amen.**

(See hymn No. 3.)

Fourth Sunday of Advent

Old Testament: 2 Samuel 7:8–16
Psalm 89:1–4, 19–24
Epistle: Romans 16:25–27
Gospel: Luke 1:26–38

CALL TO WORSHIP

God has appointed for us places and responsibilities.
Come now to claim what God has entrusted to us.
We hear God calling us, and we seek to respond.
We feel God's presence and sense God's purposes.
In steadfast love and faithfulness
God keeps covenant with us.
We gather together to remember that God rules,
that nothing in our lives is beyond God's care.
No enemies within or without can affect or disturb
when we turn to the One who strengthens us.
We turn away from violence, troubles, and fear
to seek God's revelation and sing our Creator's praise.
Amen. **Amen.**

INVOCATION

Eternal God, who raised up our ancestors to recognize and affirm their
chosenness, help us to see in ourselves the sacred value we have as your
children. Turn us away from all that diminishes and destroys the persons
you have created us to be. Establish your reign within us and among us,
for no other ruler can bring out our best or help us deal effectively with
present realities in our world. May our worship proclaim your steadfast
love and faithfulness. Amen.

CALL TO CONFESSION

Again, in this Advent Season we are summoned to prepare for God's
coming to us in a form we can begin to understand. Jesus accepted all our
human limitations yet remained faithful to the Eternal law of love. We
who have taken this saving action for granted are called to repent and be
watchful. Let us confess our disobedience.

PRAYER OF CONFESSION

Great God of All Worlds, we have denied your rule and ignored your
purposes. We have forgotten what it means to live as a covenant people,
for we have gone our own way, viewing others of your children as
enemies. Break down our resistance to the leading of your Spirit. Forgive

our waywardness, and give us courage to pray that all may be done to us according to your will. Amen.

ASSURANCE OF FORGIVENESS
You have found favor with God, who, in steadfast love and faithfulness, claims you even when you go your own way. God calls you by name and, with discipline and protection, restores you to the family of faith. Renew for yourselves the covenant vision by which our spiritual ancestors have lived. Amen.

COLLECT
God of All Mystery, whom we have glimpsed in Christ Jesus, extend your revelation to us today. Draw us deeper into covenant with you, sustaining us by your steadfast love and faithfulness. May we know your discipline and your favor, both in worship and in our daily living. Amen.

OFFERTORY INVITATION
By amazing grace we have received the gifts we are about to share. All that we give—and all that we retain for our own use—is claimed by God. May we bring our offerings and ourselves to proclaim good news of Advent for our own day.

OFFERTORY PRAYER
For your love, protection, and discipline, we give thanks, O God. In gratitude we bring the work of our hands for your blessing. May all the efforts supported by these offerings carry forward your vision for the world. Accomplish through these gifts and our attempts to be faithful that which is impossible by human design alone. Amen.

COMMISSION AND BLESSING
God sends us out, empowered by the gospel,
to fill our appointed roles among God's people.
   We will go where God sends us,
   alert to the voice and vision of our Creator.
No matter where we go we are not alone,
for God has chosen to live in covenant with us.
   We welcome God's rule in our daily lives
   and open ourselves to God's continuing revelation.
Receive and claim the strength God promises.
Live by the faith entrusted to you for sharing.
   In obedience and joy we pass on to others
   the love we have received from our Maker.
Amen.   **Amen.**

(See hymn No. 4.)

The Christmas Season

Christmas Eve/Day

Old Testament: Isaiah 9:2–7
Psalm 96
Epistle: Titus 2:11–14
Gospel: Luke 2:1–20

CALL TO WORSHIP

Sing a new song, all the earth,
for God's gift of light and love.
Bless God's name and proclaim God's salvation.
"Glory to God in the highest!"
Unto us a child is born;
in a manger the grace of God appears.
The baby, for whom there was no room,
welcomes us to honored places in God's family.
Declare God's marvelous works;
honor God with your thanksgiving and praise.
We rejoice in Christ's coming
and give thanks for the love God reveals.

INVOCATION

Mighty God, whose saving grace is revealed in unexpected times and
places, invade our routines and penetrate our bland expectations. Come
to us here in such glory and power that we cannot miss your visitation.
Confront us with your truth and awaken us with your righteous judgment. In the name of Bethlehem's Babe, who lived to save us from
ourselves. Amen.

CALL TO CONFESSION

Come out of the shadows into God's light. Leave behind the limitations of
your own narrow experience to venture into the vast unknown reaches of
God's love. Renounce all that creates barriers and protected isolation, to
find the community God intends. Open your hearts that your sin might
be forgiven and your soul find release.

PRAYER OF CONFESSION

Everlasting One, whose glory and majesty we dare to approach only with
fear and trembling, hear our cries. We are poor and needy in spite of your
generous mercy, for we have followed our own passions and tried to shape
our destinies with our own hands. We have created structures and pro-
cedures to secure and protect advantages for ourselves. We have ignored

the signs of your presence and denied the evidence of your righteous judgment. Forgive us, Mighty God, and strengthen us for fuller service. In Jesus' name. Amen.

ASSURANCE OF FORGIVENESS

God judges with equity and righteousness. Our Maker equips us to live according to the truth. All oppressive burdens we have known are lightened by the One who bore our sins and carries our sorrows. The grace of God has appeared for our salvation. The gift of God's peace is granted to those who embrace justice. We are empowered to sing a new song and to declare God's marvelous works. Amen.

COLLECT

We who live in the midst of wars and rumors of wars, who see oppression, self-centeredness, and brokenness on every hand, look to you, O God, to intervene. Let us hear again the promises of broken yokes and blessed hopes. Assure us that trampling warriors and oppressive rulers do not have the last word. Send to us once more the Wonderful Counselor and Prince of Peace, in whose name we pray. Amen.

OFFERTORY INVITATION

"Ascribe to God the glory due God's name; bring an offering, and come into God's courts." Bring your material gifts to honor God. Offer here your time and effort, that God's truth may be proclaimed. We have been richly blessed; now it is our privilege to share.

OFFERTORY PRAYER

May these gifts of time, talent, and treasure proclaim your saving action in Jesus Christ. Through our offerings empower this church to share the good news we have seen and heard. Equip us to sing with angels and run with shepherds. Fill us with your peace, that we may live more fully as peacemakers. Expand the horizons of our understanding and expectation, that we may move with confidence into those wider arenas where you call us to serve. In the name of Jesus. Amen.

COMMISSION AND BLESSING

When we are together, it is easy to believe
the songs, promises, and hope of Christmas.
   We are filled with expectation and trust;
   surely God is acting to change our world.
But as we scatter, the vision dims in a cruel world
where peace and justice do not reign.
   We carry with us apprehension and doubt
   as God calls us to be instruments of a just peace.
Accept the empowerment of God's grace.
Know that God goes with you as you serve.

We receive, with joy and trembling, our commission
to sing a new song in all the earth.
Amen.   **Amen.**

(See hymns No. 5 and No. 6.)

Christmas Day
(Alternate Reading 1)

Old Testament: Isaiah 62:6–7, 10–12
                   Psalm 97
Epistle: Titus 3:4–7
Gospel: Luke 2:8–20

CALL TO WORSHIP

Come, all who await God's coming;
there is good news of great joy!
God has come among us
in a baby of humble birth.
Our salvation has come;
let heaven and earth rejoice!
Give thanks to God's holy name,
for God's light has dawned among us.
Join the multitudes who sing,
"Glory to God in the highest."
God has redeemed us and calmed our fears;
we are God's own, sought out and not forsaken.

INVOCATION

Great God of All the Universe, before you all our idols are broken down
in their insignificance. All the treasures of earth, which we cherish,
become as dust. You who rule beyond the far reaches of time and space
come now to reign within us. Lift us up to your light and joy. Speak to us
that we may hear and be glad. Amen.

CALL TO CONFESSION

In the presence of One before whom mountains melt and the earth
trembles, we come now to rid ourselves of all that separates us from God
and our best selves. Let us open our hearts to God's light and truth, as we
confess our sin.

PRAYER OF CONFESSION

Eternal One, our eyes have focused for so long on what is temporary that
we cannot see the signs of your everlasting presence and activity. We have

bowed down before idols of our own making and systems of our own design. They have become for us so powerful and compelling that we forget who you are. Our questions are silenced, our petitions go unexpressed, and faith becomes a hollow form with no substance. In our self-centeredness we are reduced to a mere shadow of the potential you placed within us. Turn us around, God, for we cannot save ourselves. Amen.

ASSURANCE OF FORGIVENESS
"When the goodness and loving kindness of God our Savior appeared, we were saved, not because of deeds done by us in righteousness, but in virtue of God's own mercy, by the washing of regeneration and renewal in the Holy Spirit, which God poured out upon us richly through Jesus Christ our Savior, so that we might be justified by God's grace and become heirs in hope of eternal life."
God has forgiven us. Let us live as forgiven people. Amen.

COLLECT
Preserver of Life, enlist us among your saints, to watch and serve and build. Open our ears to good news. Open our lips to share it. Open our hearts to embrace all whom you call us to love. In Jesus' name. Amen.

OFFERTORY INVITATION
This time of sharing is our opportunity to give thanks to God. It provides a way for us to identify with the saving activity of our Creator among us. It prompts us to clear away stones and build highways, that others may come to know the joy of participation in God's promises. Let us join in this privileged act of giving with all we have and are.

OFFERTORY PRAYER
In light of your gift at Bethlehem, we have not yet begun to give. But we bring to you this portion of all you give us to manage, asking that you will use it, through your church, to bring about the good you intend. We would glorify and praise you in our gifts of time and talent, as well as treasure. Amen.

COMMISSION AND BLESSING
Go forth into the world to share the song,
"Glory to God in the highest!"
God is alive in us and in our world.
God rules over all time and space.
Let all the earth hear of God's salvation:
"Peace on earth; good will to all people."
God calls us away from evil to do good.
God invites us to be saints and deliverers.
Go in confidence, for God is with you,
offering grace, mercy, and peace.

We are not alone; we are not afraid.
We are renewed; thanks be to God!
Amen.   Amen.

(See hymn No. 7.)

Christmas Day
(Alternate Reading 2)

Old Testament: Isaiah 52:7–10
Psalm 98
Epistle: Hebrews 1:1–12
Gospel: John 1:1–14

CALL TO WORSHIP
Come to hear the good news of Christmas;
Rejoice in the light Christ brings.
Christ unfolds before us the abundant life.
We rejoice in the Word-made-flesh.
Sing a new song of steadfast love and faithfulness.
Rejoice in the good tidings of salvation.
God reigns! Let all the earth sing for joy.
We rejoice in God's victory and in our redemption.
Worship our God, who brings comfort and healing.
Rejoice in the new life that is ours.
God's peace was lived out in Jesus of Nazareth;
We rejoice in the Human One, full of grace and truth.

INVOCATION
Ruler of All Worlds, come to reign within and among us, as we seek to watch with you in this holy hour. All the hills burst into singing before the greatest of all your gifts to us. Grant that we may know Jesus in all the fullness of glory with which you surround your lived Word. Stir us with your winds and flames of fire. Make us your partners in serving all the worlds' people. In Jesus' name. Amen.

CALL TO CONFESSION
Come away from dull routines to experience anew the Power that transcends and encompasses all space and time. All nature and humanity pause before the Creator in awe and wonder that God cares. Our lives can be right with God only as we strip away the barrier we erect against God's reign. Let us admit the sham and pretension within so we can get on with true and meaningful existence.

PRAYER OF CONFESSION

O God, we have heard your prophets and ignored their message. We have met Jesus of Nazareth and tried to reduce his words and deeds to fit our own desires. We have talked about love but reserved its practice for times when we felt like sharing it, with those who met our criteria. We welcome again your good tidings of peace, but we are not ready to give up the swords we have hidden away for our own defense. We rejoice in the good news that we are all your children, in Christ, but we prefer to think we have a special claim on your care. We ask for your forgiveness and seek your healing. In Jesus' name. Amen.

ASSURANCE OF FORGIVENESS

The ends of the earth see God's salvation. Mountains and hills clap their hands and sing for joy. Jesus Christ has achieved our forgiveness and purification. Let us receive God's gift and believe. Let us give thanks for light and life, and share them. In Jesus' name. Amen.

COLLECT

As you have spoken through the prophets and in the birth of a child, O God of All the Universe, come to us now through the people and events surrounding our lives. May your Word in Jesus of Nazareth be alive in the church, which seeks to extend Christ's ministry. With all nature and with a mighty chorus of angels and servants, may we break forth into singing as we receive your good news. Amen.

OFFERTORY INVITATION

We have often failed to acknowledge gifts we have received from God. In truth, we have refused to receive Christ as God's Word-made-flesh. But it is not too late to change our ways. In this present moment we have the opportunity to express our thanks in a new level of commitment and giving. Those who truly believe cannot help but be grateful and generous. Let us give as God has blessed us.

OFFERTORY PRAYER

We bring these offerings, O God, to further your rule among us. We dedicate them to your honor and glory and to the service of humankind. May they carry your light to a shadowed and weary world. May they proclaim your truth amid the lies in which your people live. May they herald your victory among all who truly seek a better way. Amen.

COMMISSION AND BLESSING

Go forth to share the good news of Christmas;
carry to others the light Christ has brought.
   We want to live the abundant life,
   revealed to us in the Word-made-flesh.
Convey to all, God's steadfast love and faithfulness;
live as people who are being healed.

We want the rule of God to shape all we do;
we want our lives to reflect the love of Jesus.
Take with you the assurance of comfort and peace;
know that you have received God's blessing.
We rejoice in grace and truth granted us in Jesus,
as we reach for our full humanity in Christ.
Amen.   Amen.

(See hymn No. 8.)

Christmas 1

Old Testament: Isaiah 61:10—62:3
                Psalm 111
Epistle: Galatians 4:4–7
Gospel: Luke 2:22–40

CALL TO WORSHIP
Let us rejoice in God, our Sovereign,
whose salvation comes in everyday events.
In the face of a child God is revealed.
In the babe of Bethlehem we are healed.
Let us give thanks with our whole hearts,
for God is gracious and merciful.
In the food we eat God's love is shown.
As the bread is broken our worth is known.
Let us worship the God of wondrous works,
who offers to enter into covenant with us.
In the gift of Christ we receive a new name;
salvation comes and nothing is the same.

INVOCATION
Sovereign God, who visited this planet in Jesus of Nazareth, renew within us the sense of your presence with us. We give thanks for your works of love and your merciful provision for all our needs. In covenant with you and all your people, we join in worship and service. In the name of Jesus Christ. Amen.

CALL TO CONFESSION
From the boundless mercy of God we have received courage to address the Almighty, who judges but also redeems, who has created us to live fully in this present moment but has also planted eternity in our minds.

Before this good and gracious God we pour out our confession. Let us pray.

PRAYER OF CONFESSION

Eternal One, we have neglected to look for signs of your presence, so we have not seen your works. We organize life for our own self-interest, so we have failed to find you in the people and events surrounding us. Our worship is filled with empty words, while our hearts are closed to your transforming Spirit. Even the wonder of new life leaves us unmoved. Break into our routine dullness to forgive and change us. Rename us, and make us whole. Amen.

ASSURANCE OF FORGIVENESS

In light, truth, and grace God surrounds us with a love that will not let us go, turning our mourning into joy, our sin into forgiveness, freedom, and wholeness, our fear into awe, wonder, and rejoicing. Today God calls us each by name, welcomes us into the family of faith, and grants us peace that the world cannot give. Thanks be to God! Amen.

COLLECT

In these awesome moments we await your truth, O God. You are far beyond the words we will hear, but these words can be the carrier of yours. Be as real to us as you were to our biblical ancestors. Grant us eyes to see your salvation and true commitment to the covenant you have made with us. Open our lips to share with one another and the whole world the insights and experience you grant us. Amen.

OFFERTORY INVITATION

Remember the wonderful works of God, and give thanks. Remember God's generous provision for you as you bring your gifts of time, talents, and treasure. May our offerings be a channel for God's continuing revelation.

OFFERTORY PRAYER

As the parents of Jesus brought sacrifices to honor you, O God, we would give our best for the witness and outreach of your church. May you be honored in all our actions, not just in these gifts. May our daily work praise you, our family life glorify you, and all our thoughts reflect your will for us. In Jesus' name. Amen.

COMMISSION AND BLESSING

In our coming together we know God in new ways.
We sustain one another in our mutual covenant.
As we part, God goes with us
and the ties that bind us to one another continue.
God has named us and redeemed us.
Our eyes have been open to see God's salvation.

The thoughts of our hearts have been revealed,
and God has clothed us with righteousness.
Depart now in God's peace,
sharing that peace with all your worlds.
**We will not keep silent, but will speak
and act according to God's word.**
Amen.   **Amen.**

(See hymns No. 9 and No. 10.)

January 1
(New Year)

Old Testament: Ecclesiastes 3:1–13
                 Psalm 8
Epistle: Colossians 2:1–7
Gospel: Matthew 9:14–17

CALL TO WORSHIP

Come, let us close the doors to our past
that we might enter fully into God's new day.
**We pause in the midst of time
to ponder the vast reaches of eternity.**
For everything there is a season:
a time to mourn and weep, a time to dance and laugh.
**God has made everything beautiful;
how wonderful, beyond our knowing, are all God's works!**
How majestic is God's name in all the earth!
How amazing is God's care for us!
**We rejoice in the faith we have received
and give thanks to God as we have been taught.**

INVOCATION

O God, who makes all things new, we come to you in these times of
hatred, killing, war, and losing to claim your gifts of love, healing, peace,
and aspiration. You have promised us that you care, and our hearts are
encouraged. You have made us a little less than God, and we are filled
with awe. You have called us from our fasting to feast with you in your
own new day. Enliven all our senses to appreciate the moments before us
and awaken us to your guiding love. Amen.

CALL TO CONFESSION

From the boundless mercy of God we have received courage to address the Almighty, who judges but also redeems, who has created us to live fully in this present moment but has also planted eternity in our minds. Before this good and gracious God, we pour out our confession. Let us pray.

PRAYER OF CONFESSION

God of Majesty and Freshness, we confess our failure to reach for either perfection or renewal. We have been content with old wineskins and tired formulas. We have resisted change and challenge, denying the grand possibilities of our humanity and turning our backs on the abundant life Christ offers. With eyes that do not see, we miss the vision of the heavens and the glory of serving in Christ's name. Forgive us and restore us to the roles you have planned for us in your world. Amen.

ASSURANCE OF FORGIVENESS

In light, truth, and grace God surrounds us with a love that will not let us go, turning our mourning into joy, our sin into forgiveness, freedom, and wholeness, our fear into awe, wonder and rejoicing. Today God calls us each by name, welcomes us into the family of faith, and grants us peace that the world cannot give. Thanks be to God! Amen.

COLLECT

Through all the seasons of life you are with us, O God, to knit us together in mutual love and caring. You pour out abundant gifts that enrich our existence and challenge us to give our best. As we hear and reflect on your word, establish us in the faith and teach us to be warm, thankful, and happy mirrors of your divine intention. In Jesus' name. Amen.

OFFERTORY INVITATION

What have we gained for our toil? Pause to consider the abundant mercies of God in our lives. We have not earned them. All our striving can reveal only glimpses of the mystery of God. But as we live in Christ we are moved to continuous thanksgiving. May that gratitude be reflected in our giving.

OFFERTORY PRAYER

God of All Majesty and Glory, receive our outpouring of love in these gifts and in our renewed commitment to your purposes. For all the beauty in nature and people that you have provided we give thanks. May riches of understanding abound, the more we give, and treasures of wisdom flow through us and our church to enlighten a troubled and needy world. In Jesus' name. Amen.

COMMISSION AND BLESSING

Enter the new year, rejoicing in its opportunities
and facing its challenges with faith.

We want to live fully every moment,
embracing eternity in the midst of time.
Amid the hating, wars, and casting of stones,
welcome love, peace, and times of gathering.
**Amid losing, rending, and painful silence,
we will seek, sew, and speak of love.**
Go out in confidence and joy,
for God crowns you with glory and honor.
**We will rejoice in Christ's presence with us
and join the celebration of God's love.**
Amen.   **Amen.**

(See hymn No. 11.)

January 1
(Celebration of Jesus and Mary)

Old Testament: Numbers 6:22–27
                 Psalm 67
Epistle: Philippians 2:9–13 (alt.)
                 Galatians 4:4–7
Gospel: Luke 2:15–21

CALL TO WORSHIP
Be glad, sing for joy, all humankind;
God calls you by name, and blesses you.
**Let all the people praise you, O God.
Let all people praise your holy name.**
God sent Jesus to witness among us
and exalted Jesus' name above all others.
**In Christ, God's way is known on earth,
God's saving power among all the nations.**
In the meditation and trust of Mary
all human pretensions find their proper focus.
**We open ourselves to this movement of God's Spirit
and bow our knees to confess our faith in Christ.**

INVOCATION
Holy God, with us in all times and places, become real to us here as,
together, we seek to be in touch with your purposes and attuned to your
leading. Fill us with good news we can share in all the Bethlehems of our
own day. Let your face shine upon us to bless us. In Jesus' name. Amen.

CALL TO CONFESSION

From the boundless mercy of God we have received courage to address the Almighty, who judges but also redeems, who has created us to live fully in this present moment but has also planted eternity in our minds. Before this good and gracious God we pour out our confession. Let us pray.

PRAYER OF CONFESSION

God of All Mercy, forgive us, for we have not worked at issues of salvation. We have ignored you rather than tremble before you. We have resisted you rather than open ourselves to work for your good pleasure. We have slept through your revelation and kept quiet when we should have spoken. Hear our prayers and release us to become what you intend for us to be. In Jesus' name. Amen.

ASSURANCE OF FORGIVENESS

In light, truth, and grace God surrounds us with a love that will not let us go, turning our mourning into joy, our sin into forgiveness, freedom, and wholeness, our fear into awe, wonder, and rejoicing. Today God calls each of us by name, welcomes us into the family of faith, and grants us peace that the world cannot give. Thanks be to God! Amen.

COLLECT

Lift up your countenance upon us, Gracious God, that we may know your saving power and be equipped for obedient service. Let your work be done in us, in our times of reflection and in all the occasions that call for action. May our faithfulness increase as we hear and heed your word. Amen.

OFFERTORY INVITATION

The earth has yielded its increase, and God has blessed us. We have more to give than we have ever dared to share. May what we bring today be used to fulfill God's intent for us and our neighbors, near and far.

OFFERTORY PRAYER

Thank you, God, for your generous blessings that lift us above the mundane to know true spiritual discernment. Shine the beacon of your love in and through these gifts, that your saving way may be known on earth and your peace rest on all your children. Amen.

COMMISSION AND BLESSING

Carry your gladness and joy into the world,
where God's name is not cherished or honored.
   **We will sing God's praise by the way we live
   and invite others to join in the song.**
Exalting the name of Jesus Christ,
make your witness to the least and the greatest.

As Jesus met people where they were,
we will seek to identify with all we encounter.
God will bless you and keep you;
the face of the Eternal will shine on you.
We rejoice in the peace God offers
and welcome the guidance God gives.
Amen.   Amen.

(See hymn No. 12.)

Christmas 2

Old Testament: Jeremiah 31:7–14
                    Psalm 147:12–20
Epistle: Ephesians 1:3–6, 15–18
Gospel: John 1:1–18

CALL TO WORSHIP

Praise God, who protects and blesses us,
who waters our lives like a garden.
Thanks be to God for cool, refreshing water,
for grain, oil, wine, and flocks.
Sing for joy that a remnant responds
and joins in the growth faith demands.
We would dare to listen and hear God's voice,
to rejoice with dance and merrymaking.
Join the saints in prayers of remembrance
and look forward in your call to hope.
God meets us in our celebration
and enlightens the eyes of our hearts.
Amen.   Amen.

INVOCATION

Bring us together from our far places, O God, whether the separation be
that of physical or of emotional distance. Unite men, women, and children in your worship—old and young and in between. Minister to the
brokenhearted among us and lift up the fallen. May we know the consolation you intend for all your people, and the gladness that comes unbidden
as we serve you. In Jesus' name. Amen.

CALL TO CONFESSION

From the boundless mercy of God we have received courage to address
the Almighty, who judges but also redeems, who has created us to live

fully in the present moment but has also planted eternity in our minds. Before this good and gracious God we pour out our confession. Let us pray.

PRAYER OF CONFESSION
Almighty God, we have turned from your way and stumbled through life, intent on our own pursuits. We have rejected the witness of those whom we envy or fear, and dismissed the revelation of Jesus as too visionary and demanding. We have received the earth's abundance from your hand as if it were our due, and rejected spiritual blessings as impractical and unworthy of our notice. Forgive our foolishness, O God, and destine us in love to live as your children, through Christ. Amen.

ASSURANCE OF FORGIVENESS
In light, truth, and grace God surrounds us with a love that will not let us go, turning our mourning into joy, our sin into forgiveness, freedom, and wholeness, our fear into awe, wonder, and rejoicing. Today God calls us each by name, welcomes us into the family of faith, and grants us peace that the world cannot give. Thanks be to God! Amen.

COLLECT
Fill us with radiant joy as your word runs swiftly through our midst, melting the coldness of our hearts and bringing light to the darkness of our souls. Quicken our faith in Jesus Christ, who reveals to us your will and way. May the statutes and ordinances that have guided your people in the past find a friendly reception among those seeking to embrace your revelation and grow in love. Through Christ. Amen.

OFFERTORY INVITATION
We give because we want the church to be here when we need it. We give because God wants the church to be wherever people are in need. Let us be as generous in our sharing as God has been with us.

OFFERTORY PRAYER
May these gifts bear testimony to the light we have received in Jesus Christ. May the grace and truth, communicated to us, be shared with others. Bless and multiply our giving, to your honor and glory and the service of all humankind. Amen.

COMMISSION AND BLESSING
Continue your worship in daily praise,
giving thanks for material and spiritual gifts.
> **Praise God for all we have received**
> **and for all we are privileged to share.**
Join the remnant of God's people
who are growing in grace and truth.
> **We dare to join the dance of life**

without stopping to count the cost.
The promise and blessing of an unseen God
go with you and be seen by you.
Open our eyes, O God, to the view beyond us,
and fill us with the fullness of Christ.
Amen.   **Amen.**

(See hymn No. 13.)

The Epiphany Season

Epiphany

Old Testament: Isaiah 60:1–6
Psalm 72:1–14
Epistle: Ephesians 3:1–12
Gospel: Matthew 2:1–12

CALL TO WORSHIP   1/1/89

Have you seen the star of Bethlehem?
Arise, people of God; let it shine in your lives.
We have seen Christ's star and have come to worship.
We are ready to let God lead and direct us.
Come from the shadows of earth
to the light of God's eternal purposes.
We see the glory of God in our midst
and our hearts rejoice in expectation.
The promises of the gospel are for us,
and for all people everywhere.
We are here to be equipped by God
to carry good news into the world.
all: **Amen.   Amen.**

INVOCATION   1/1/89

We come to your light, God of All History, seeking to experience your
presence at work among us and within each one. In our poverty of spirit
we reach for the unsearchable riches of Christ. Amid our narrowness of
vision we long for an outpouring of your all-inclusive love. From our
advantaged position in your world we seek to develop greater compassion
for the needy and oppressed. Move us from our complacency to be and
do more fully as you intend. Amen.

CALL TO CONFESSION

Lift your eyes to see the mercy of our God. We need not carry the guilt
that is in us, day after day. God is willing to knit the fragmented pieces of
our existence into a meaningful whole. Let us pour out our need for
pardon, trusting God's mercy.

PRAYER OF CONFESSION

Just and Righteous Ruler, we bring to you our good intentions and our
poor follow-through. We want to live in the light, yet we continue to
dwell content in the shadows, where less seems to be demanded of us.
We desire to identify with the poor and help to win justice for them, but

25

sometimes they seem a threat to our values and advantages. We pray for peace and yet tolerate whatever violence seems to offer us protection. Forgive our duplicity and restore us to single-minded devotion to your compassionate will, through Christ. Amen.

ASSURANCE OF FORGIVENESS

God's grace and power transformed Paul from a tyrannical persecutor to an effective witness to the gospel. God offers to bridge the distance between our aims and our achievements, and is ready to use our gifts in service to a needy world. Thanks be to God for healing our fragmented lives and empowering our witness. Amen.

COLLECT

Shine your truth into our lives, O God, sharpening our awareness of your abundant gifts and attuning us to the signs by which you would lead us. As heirs of your promise, we seek to be guided by your eternal purposes, that the church may make your wisdom known. Through Christ. Amen.

OFFERTORY INVITATION

Abundance and wealth have come to us, that we might experience the privilege of sharing. Christ, who often had nowhere to lay his head, gave life itself to unfold before us the way of life. As we share what we have received, our lives are opened to appreciate and enjoy more of God's blessings. Let us bring our offerings to God.

OFFERTORY PRAYER

O God, from whom comes all the good things we enjoy, we offer our gifts in the spirit of those long ago who opened costly treasures before Jesus. We give in response to your generosity, identifying with your pity and compassion for victims of violence, poverty, and oppression. May all who are in need experience the unsearchable riches of Christ and the gift of the Holy Spirit, even as their physical needs are met. May we be co-workers with Christ, whose sacrifice bought our redemption. Amen.

COMMISSION AND BLESSING

The light of God's purposes has shone upon us.
Carry that light into another week.
**The star of God's promises that led us to worship
now leads us to serve in God's world.**
When we have met God in the light,
We cannot dwell comfortably in the shadows.
**We cannot enjoy our abundance and wealth
without thanksgiving and generous sharing.**
The glory of God shines on you today.
Others will see your radiance and rejoice with you.

We seek God's peace that we may share it,
God's wisdom that we may live by it.
In Christ's name.
Amen.   **Amen.**

(See hymn No. 14.)

First Sunday After Epiphany
(Baptism of Our Sovereign)

Old Testament: Genesis 1:1–5
             Psalm 29
Epistle: Acts 19:1–7
Gospel: Mark 1:4–11

CALL TO WORSHIP
God, of the whirlwind and fire,
sweeps into our presence in this hour.
Glory be to God, who strengthens us
and blesses all people with peace.
God, who called all worlds into being,
calls forth new life in us today.
Glory be to God, in whose creative
purpose we are claimed and empowered.
God, whose Spirit unites all people in a common
language of love, *of the Spirit*
confirms God's gifts in us as we gather here.
Glory be to God who created light in which
we can walk in confident expectation.

INVOCATION
Glory be to you, O God, whom we worship in awe and wonder. You are
the author of all beginnings and all that is pronounced "good." In you
both day and night have purpose, both calm and storm have meaning.
Open the eyes of our imagination that we may be ready to receive your
gifts and discern your activity in our midst. In the name of Jesus, in
whose baptism we, too, are baptized. Amen.

CALL TO CONFESSION
Come, beloved children of God, in the name of one who embodied
humanity according to God's purposes. Come to confess your sin, to
acknowledge all that separates you from the Creator of Life. May our

The Epiphany Season   27

words and the quiet longing of our hearts open our lives to welcome active encounter with the God who loves us. Let us pray.

PRAYER OF CONFESSION

Creator of All Worlds, we confess to sporadic beliefs and inconsistent faithfulness. Before the mystery of the universe our minds cannot grasp a God who embraces infinity. In the face of natural disasters and cruel inhumanity we doubt that Love reigns. Between our own actions and the best we know we see a wide gap that we cannot bridge. O God, reclaim us, and help us to reclaim our baptism; we need your healing, forgiving, transforming Spirit. Amen.

ASSURANCE OF FORGIVENESS

God grants us baptism with water and the Holy Spirit. We are forgiven; we are loved; we are empowered. May God bless us with peace. Amen.

COLLECT

Great God, who baptized Jesus and confirmed in your early disciples the gifts of the Spirit, grant us to hear and see your creative movement among us. Make your voice plain as you strengthen us to face the problems and possibilities of life. Grant us your strength and bless us with peace. Amen.

OFFERTORY INVITATION

Abundance and wealth have come to us, that we might experience the privilege of sharing. Christ, who often had nowhere to lay his head, gave life itself to unfold before us the way of life. As we share what we have received, our lives are opened to appreciate and enjoy more of God's blessings. Let us bring our offerings to God.

OFFERTORY PRAYER

O God, from whom comes all the good things we enjoy, we offer our gifts in the spirit of those long ago who opened costly treasures before Jesus. We give in response to your generosity, identifying with your pity and compassion for victims of violence, poverty, and oppression. May all who are in need experience the unsearchable riches of Christ and the gift of the Holy Spirit, even as their physical needs are met. May we be co-workers with Christ, whose sacrifice bought our redemption. Amen.

COMMISSION AND BLESSING

The peace of God, known in this sanctuary,
go with you, empowering you to meet adversity.
We carry God's peace into a troubled world,
seeking to be peacemakers wherever we go.
The blessing of God, who touched believers' lips
and set them free to sing praises,
lift you up each day to use your gifts.

We carry God's blessing into our daily lives
and dare to share the riches entrusted to us.
The strength of God, seen in wind and fire,
set you ablaze with vitality and purpose.
We commit ourselves anew to live by God's will
as it is revealed to us day by day.
Amen.   **Amen.**

(See hymn No. 15.)

Second Sunday After Epiphany

Old Testament: 1 Samuel 3:1–10 (11–20)
                        Psalm 63:1–8
Epistle: Romans 16:1–7 (alt.)
                        1 Corinthians 6:12–15a, 19–20
Gospel: John 1:35–42

CALL TO WORSHIP
Come to hear God's call to service;
come to meet the Christ who claims you.
Speak, O God, for your servant hears.
Show us the way, for we would follow.
Come, responding to God's summons.
Come, rejoicing that God cares.
With longing hearts we seek God's love;
with joyful lips we sing God's praise.
Come, for we are not our own.
God's love, in Christ, has made us saints.
God is our help and our support;
nothing we have done can cut off our Creator's care.

INVOCATION
God of All Our Moments, day and night, awaken us to hear what you
would say to us. Help us to know when it is your voice we are hearing and
when it is our own prejudices and desires to which we are paying heed.
We open ourselves to behold your glory in the sanctuary and to know
your steadfast love, which is better than life. Amen.

CALL TO CONFESSION
Come, all who live in prisons of limited loyalties and misplaced trust.
Come, all who are enslaved by your own passions and greed. Come, for
there is forgiveness and health for all who are truly repentant. Let us
confess our sin.

PRAYER OF CONFESSION

O Holy One, we are reluctant to turn to you. We would rather hide from your judgment and pretend that we have everything under control. We justify our ways, and we reject the standards and values you build into life, as if they were relics of a bygone era. We close ourselves off from you, and then we are swayed by those who proclaim you dead. O God, the paths we have chosen are leading us nowhere except into confusion and despair. Save us from our destructive choices, that we may reclaim the vision you set before us. Amen.

ASSURANCE OF FORGIVENESS

You are not your own; you were bought with a price. The Messiah has come, and you have been claimed as God's own. As Christ was raised from the dead, so, too, all who long to escape the death of sin are lifted by God to newness of life. Accept the pardon and transformation God offers in Christ. Amen.

COLLECT

With all your saints and ministers, we open our ears and hearts to claim the message you would speak to us. May we meditate on your word, praise you with joyful lips, and glorify you with our whole being. Come, Holy Spirit, to make your home in our midst and within each one of us, driving away all that distorts our vision. Then use us, we pray, to reach others with your saving good news. Amen.

OFFERTORY INVITATION

Abundance and wealth have come to us, that we might experience the privilege of sharing. Christ, who often had nowhere to lay his head, gave life itself to unfold before us the way of life. As we share what we have received, our lives are opened to appreciate and enjoy more of God's blessings. Let us bring our offerings to God.

OFFERTORY PRAYER

O God, from whom comes all the good things we enjoy, we offer our gifts in the spirit of those long ago who opened costly treasures before Jesus. We give in response to your generosity, identifying with your pity and compassion for victims of violence, poverty, and oppression. May all who are in need experience the unsearchable riches of Christ and the gift of the Holy Spirit, even as their physical needs are met. May we be co-workers with Christ, whose sacrifice bought our redemption. Amen.

COMMISSION AND BLESSING

Go forth to answer God's call to service,
sharing the love of Christ with all you meet.
    We have heard God's word for our day
    and want to follow where Christ leads.

Venture into unknown tomorrows in faith,
for you are co-workers with Christ.
We have found the Messiah!
All of life is made new in Jesus Christ.
You are set free from bondage and fear;
you shall be called by a new name.
We will glorify God in our bodies
and welcome the Spirit's dwelling within.
Amen.   **Amen.**

(See hymn No. 16.)

Third Sunday After Epiphany

Old Testament: Jonah 3:1–5, 10
                          Psalm 62:5–12
Epistle: 1 Corinthians 7:29–31 (32–35)
Gospel: Mark 1:14–20

CALL TO WORSHIP
Come, with undivided attention, to meet God,
who calls you away from old routines.
Our souls wait for God in silence.
We hope in God, our rock and our salvation.
Come without anxiety or fear,
for God cares for you.
We come with devotion to our Sovereign,
in whom time is fulfilled and life has meaning.
Enter the realm of God, which is here and now,
as well as beyond time and place.
We pour out our hearts before God,
whom we trust and honor.

INVOCATION
Great God, our fortress and refuge, we seek comfort and reassurance in your presence. We bring our commitments and our works before you because yours is the only standard that finally matters. We open ourselves to your direction, confident that you see value and purpose in our lives that we ourselves cannot discern. Deliver us in this hour from all that separates us from experiencing communion with you. Amen.

CALL TO CONFESSION
We, who have often turned away from God's direction and purpose, have come together to confront our disobedience and our willful disregard of

the divine intent. Despite good intentions, we have broken trust with God and with one another. Let us acknowledge our sin, that we may be open to God's healing and the restoration of right relationships with our neighbors.

PRAYER OF CONFESSION

Ever-present God, we confess that we have trusted our narrow under-standings rather than seek your will. We have taken our direction from the world rather than question the way things are ordered here. We have put our confidence in riches and worldly status. We have closed our ears to your call and, when we have heard that call, defied it. Even when we have followed we have resisted the evidence of your activity in our midst. Forgive us, Powerful One, and save us from ourselves, for Jesus' sake. Amen.

ASSURANCE OF FORGIVENESS

God withholds destruction and offers us a place in the eternal realm that is present, even in the midst of all life's distortions. The form of this world is passing away. The disproportions are being overcome in God, for whom there is no high or low estate. Believe the gospel; we are forgiven. Amen.

COLLECT

O God of Repeated Invitations and Challenges, let us hear you today. Help us to read the seriousness of the times in which we live. Divert our attention from interests that divide and misdirect our commitment. With the devotion of Christ's earliest disciples may we dare to leave all to follow. Amen.

OFFERTORY INVITATION

Abundance and wealth have come to us, that we might experience the privilege of sharing. Christ, who often had nowhere to lay his head, gave life itself to unfold before us the way of life. As we share what we have received, our lives are opened to appreciate and enjoy more of God's blessings. Let us bring our offerings to God.

OFFERTORY PRAYER

O God, from whom comes all the good things we enjoy, we offer our gifts in the spirit of those long ago who opened costly treasures before Jesus. We give in response to your generosity, identifying with your pity and compassion for victims of violence, poverty, and oppression. May all who are in need experience the unsearchable riches of Christ and the gift of the Holy Spirit, even as their physical needs are met. May we be co-workers with Christ, whose sacrifice bought our redemption. Amen.

COMMISSION AND BLESSING

The time is fulfilled; God's realm is at hand.
Set your hearts on God's new day.

In confidence and hope
we face the new life God intends for us.
Believe the good news of the gospel
and follow where Jesus leads.
With renewed devotion and trust
we declare ourselves ready to heed God's direction.
Receive the assurance of God's steadfast love,
which is constant and dependable.
In silence our souls wait for God,
that our steps may follow in Christ's way.
Amen.   **Amen.**

(See hymn No. 17.)

Fourth Sunday After Epiphany

Old Testament: Deuteronomy 18:15–20
                 Psalm 111
Epistle: 1 Corinthians 8:1–13
Gospel: Mark 1:21–28

CALL TO WORSHIP
Join the company of the upright
in praise and thanksgiving to God.
With our whole hearts we come,
marveling at the powerful works of our Creator.
God is gracious and merciful to us,
entering into covenant with all who respond.
In humility and amazement we answer,
for the authority of Christ compels us.
God calls us to a prophetic witness
and judges the truth of our words and deeds.
Out of our need for renewal and clearer vision
we are here to remember and learn.

INVOCATION
O God, whose precepts are established on the earth, be with us here to
teach and interpret. We know you as the only true God, but we do not
know enough of you to represent you faithfully. We have been freed from
sin to serve you, but we are not free enough of self-centeredness to feel
with others and know their need. We would be silent now, that we may be
purged of all that separates us from your truth. Amen.

CALL TO CONFESSION

In this season of showing forth the light of God's love in Christ, we are reminded that God's call to faithfulness involves our sisters and brothers, not just our relationship to the Eternal. Sometimes, when we feel most confident of salvation, we may be least aware of how our actions affect others. Let us come to God, confessing our continuing need.

PRAYER OF CONFESSION

Merciful God, deliver us from knowledge that puffs us up and makes us insensitive to others' needs. We confess that sometimes our freedom has offended another's conscience, and our carelessness has caused others to stumble and fall. Our actions have not been consistent with what we say we believe. Forgive us, O God, and restore us to a meaningful covenant with you and other seekers after your truth. In Jesus' name. Amen.

ASSURANCE OF FORGIVENESS

God is gracious and merciful, abounding in steadfast love. God judges, but God also forgives the contrite. The burden of your sin is taken away. Enter into the joy of your freedom in Christ. Rejoin the congregation of the redeemed, in humble service, through Christ. Amen.

COLLECT

Sovereign God, we who have dared to speak for you pause now to listen, lest we offer a message that is untrue to your intent. We take pleasure in the evidence of your justice, faithfulness, and healing power. May your love so strengthen our witness that we may never be a stumbling block to others. Help us now to be attentive to your word, as if we could hear your voice resounding through the universe. Amen.

OFFERTORY INVITATION

Abundance and wealth have come to us, that we might experience the privilege of sharing. Christ, who often had nowhere to lay his head, gave life itself to unfold before us the way of life. As we share what we have received, our lives are opened to appreciate and enjoy more of God's blessings. Let us bring our offerings to God.

OFFERTORY PRAYER

O God, from whom comes all the good things we enjoy, we offer our gifts in the spirit of those long ago who opened costly treasures before Jesus. We give in response to your generosity, identifying with your pity and compassion for victims of violence, poverty, and oppression. May all who are in need experience the unsearchable riches of Christ and the gift of the Holy Spirit, even as their physical needs are met. May we be co-workers with Christ, whose sacrifice bought our redemption. Amen.

COMMISSION AND BLESSING

Go forth into the world
to speak and live all God has commanded.

With our whole hearts we venture forth,
marveling at our Creator's majesty and power.
God has renewed with us an eternal covenant
in which we stand, and help others to stand.
In Christ we experience our wholeness
and dare to reach out to help others.
God goes with you, in love and support,
enabling you to make faithful witness.
Rejoicing in our heritage of faith,
we face another week, praising God.
Amen.   **Amen.**

(See hymn No. 18.)

Fifth Sunday After Epiphany

Old Testament: Job 7:1–7
Psalm 147:1–11
Epistle: 1 Corinthians 9:16–23
Gospel: Mark 1:29–39

CALL TO WORSHIP
God calls us from our aimless living,
from long nights of misery and hopelessness.
Early in the morning we seek God's face;
in this place apart we listen for God's word.
God offers release from oppressive laws
and sets us free to share the gospel.
In the hours of this day we would live good news,
offering God's love to all who will receive it.
Come before God in awe and thanksgiving,
grateful that God commissions us for service.
Day by day we pour out our life's breath,
hoping, by God's grace, to save some.
Amen.   **Amen.**

INVOCATION
God of Heaven and Earth, we, who bind ourselves to this world, seek a vision beyond ourselves and our immediate circumstances. Direct our thoughts toward the marvels of your creation and the vast possibilities for good that you have placed within us. Gather us to yourself and link us to one another in ways that will build up your church and empower our service. In Jesus' name. Amen.

CALL TO CONFESSION

Day after day we seem to be fighting demons, around us and inside us. When last we worshiped we resolved that things would be better with us. Now we come to this place and time of renewal, seeking once more to "clear the slate" with God and begin anew. Let us, together, confess our sin.

PRAYER OF CONFESSION

O God, we dare to come again, asking for forgiveness. Too often we have tossed and turned through nights of emptiness and awakened without hope. We have seen clouds without rejoicing over refreshing rain. We have confused freedom with license and mistaken humble service for weakness. Heal us and lift us up, we pray. Amen.

ASSURANCE OF FORGIVENESS

To the empty, God promises renewed meaning and purpose. For the downtrodden, there is hope for a brighter future. Those who search will find a Savior. All who are open to God's steadfast love will discover its recreating power. We are forgiven! Praise God! Amen.

COLLECT

Great and Powerful Creator and Sustainer, we are amazed to see the work of your hands. You have granted us breath and given us hope in your steadfast love. The necessity is laid on us to share your blessing. Empower us now by your word to receive your healing touch and pass it on. Amen.

OFFERTORY INVITATION

The gospel is freely given for our nurture and salvation. In gratitude we share the good news with others, through our offerings and our rededication of life to God's purposes. Let us join together in the celebration of giving.

OFFERTORY PRAYER

With these gifts we give thanks for release from slavery to the world's agenda. In awe and wonder we commit ourselves anew to the ministry of hope and healing that Jesus lived on earth. Use our offerings to extend Christ's mission where we cannot go, and to support this congregation in our efforts to be faithful where we are. Amen.

COMMISSION AND BLESSING

God sends us forth with clear directions
to take good news to all the world.
**As we have received God's love and care,
we want to pass it on.**
We are not bound by limitations of the law,
but claim our freedom in Christ.
We will live the good news of God's love

wherever we go, in all that we do.
The grace and peace of God go with you,
lifting you up and granting new life.
We do all for the sake of the gospel,
that we may share in its blessing.
Amen.   **Amen.**

(See hymn No. 19.)

Sixth Sunday After Epiphany

Old Testament: 2 Kings 5:1–14
                     Psalm 32
Epistle: 1 Corinthians 9:24–27
Gospel: Mark 1:40–45

CALL TO WORSHIP

Let us seek God at the beginning of the day,
that we may face its hours with eagerness.
  In times of distress we bring our prayers;
  in times of gladness we pour out our joy.
In the simple and commonplace God meets us.
Come, therefore, in humble obedience.
  We turn from the distractions of our daily striving
  to feel the quiet movement of God's Spirit.
God surrounds us with steadfast love
and touches our lives with new possibilities.
  We look to God for renewed health and wholeness
  and for the courage to go where we are sent.

INVOCATION

God of the Prophets, make yourself known to us as you did to them. Keep us from arrogance or self-seeking that erects barriers against your revelation. Keep us from presuming to know your intentions for us without seeking your counsel, or from supposing that we can teach others when we have ignored your directions. Help us to listen, and to respond according to your purposes, revealed in Jesus Christ. Amen.

CALL TO CONFESSION

God is our hiding place, not One from whom we can hide. The Almighty knows our inmost thoughts and secret sins. Let us pause to acknowledge the wrong in our thinking and acting, lest we waste away in mushrooming evil.

PRAYER OF CONFESSION

God of All People, we confess our self-centeredness and arrogance. We have seen our advantages as our just due, and evidence of your special favor. We have mistrusted others and misinterpreted their intentions. We have ignored sound instructions and failed to exert self-control. In the race of life we have sometimes given far less than our best. Turn us away from all that hurts and destroys, that we may accept your forgiving love and be transformed by it. Amen.

ASSURANCE OF FORGIVENESS

When we acknowledge our sin and confess our transgressions, God removes our guilt and forgives all our iniquity. Hear the prophet's word, "Wash and be clean." Amen.

COLLECT

Great God of All Times and Places, take from us our inability or unwillingness to understand your simple, straightforward message for us. May we be open to Christ's healing touch and responsive to your direction. Lead us to trust your steadfast love and accept your abundant grace. Amen.

OFFERTORY INVITATION

Make your offerings in thanksgiving for God's healing presence in your lives. Give as you have been blessed, trusting God's continuing provision for your needs.

OFFERTORY PRAYER

For the many times you have preserved us from troubles and encompassed us with deliverance, we give thanks, O God! So bless these tokens of our gratitude that we may grow in appreciation of your gifts to us and in our response to your love. May all who are helped through our offerings be led to know the blessing of community and commitment. In Christ, we would offer our best. Amen.

COMMISSION AND BLESSING

Continue in God's presence as we go our separate ways,
for we are surrounded by God's love and care.
We take with us the joy of worship and prayer
as we face the distress and distractions of the world.
There is nowhere we can go away from God
and no situation in which God is unavailable to us.
In the quiet movement of God's Spirit
we are strengthened for each day's decisions and tasks.
Face the new possibilities God offers with expectant trust,
for there is healing and hope for each day's need.
We embrace the wholeness God has revealed
and claim the courage to follow where Christ leads.
Amen.   **Amen.**

(See hymn No. 20.)

Seventh Sunday After Epiphany

Old Testament: Isaiah 43:18–25
Psalm 41
Epistle: 2 Corinthians 1:18–22
Gospel: Mark 2:1–12

CALL TO WORSHIP

God promises a new day
for those who respond to God's call.
Praise God for refreshing water
and the nourishment of bread.
God establishes and commissions us,
sending the Spirit into our hearts.
Praise God for cleansing and renewal
as we receive the bread of life.
God equips us for a life of service
among our sisters and brothers.
Praise God for meaningful work
and for the strength to respond faithfully.
Amen. **Amen.**

INVOCATION

God of Compassion and Surprises, raise our expectations so we will not miss the new things you have in store for us. Help us to see realities we have previously ignored and to hear truths we have never before discerned. Be gracious to us in this hour of worship and put your seal on us, that your glory may be revealed among us. Amen.

CALL TO CONFESSION

We, whose eyes have been closed to God's activity among us, are summoned to account for our lack of response. Have we lived as if God were irrelevant, and the needs of our sisters and brothers unimportant? Then we need to seek the grace, forgiveness, and strength God promises. Bow with me now in humble confession.

PRAYER OF CONFESSION

O God, be gracious to us, for we have sinned against you. In our busyness we have failed to call on you. In our self-centeredness we have ignored your hurting people. We have uttered empty words and wearied you with empty deeds. We have been unwilling to see our own iniquity and have not dared to believe that you can heal us. Come to us now to forgive and make new. Amen.

ASSURANCE OF FORGIVENESS

Through the prophet, God assures us: "I am the One who blots out your transgressions for my own sake, and I will not remember your sins." To the one who was paralyzed, Jesus said, "My child, your sins are forgiven. . . . Rise, take up your bed and walk." Dare to believe that you are forgiven, your sins blotted out and forgotten. Amazing grace has been offered you. Receive God's promise, and live! Amen.

COLLECT

Amazing God, we would glorify you in our listening that our words and deeds might become consistent with your will for us. We want to drink from the fountains of your love so that care for the poor becomes our rallying cry and purpose. Help us to discern the new thing you want to accomplish among us and through us. Empower us to respond with a resounding yes to your direction. Amen.

OFFERTORY INVITATION

Our offerings honor God, who has entrusted the earth's resources to our care and keeping. Through this act of giving, our personal priorities and congregational commitments are held up to the mirror of eternal values. Let us give as we have been blessed, and spend our resources that lives may be healed in Christ's name.

OFFERTORY PRAYER

Generous and Patient God, we bring our offerings with thanksgiving and our sacrifices with joy. Thank you for the privilege of sharing with those who need what we have to give. We dedicate these offerings to your glory and ourselves to your service. Amen.

COMMISSION AND BLESSING

As we face the perils and problems of a new week,
we are promised the Spirit's presence and help.
   Blessed be the Sovereign One,
   from everlasting to everlasting.
God establishes us in Christ, and commissions us
to share good news of God's healing and protection.
   God is gracious to us and will bless us
   as we minister in Christ's name.
Look forward, in joy, to the new things
God is doing in our midst.
   God blesses us day by day.
   Praise God for all life's opportunities!
Amen.   **Amen.**

(See hymn No. 21.)

Eighth Sunday After Epiphany

Old Testament: Hosea 2:14–20
Psalm 103:1–13
Epistle: 2 Corinthians 3:1–6
Gospel: Mark 2:18–22

CALL TO WORSHIP

Bless God, O my soul,
and all that is within me, bless God's holy name!
Bless God, O my soul,
and forget not all God's benefits.
God's ways, made known to people long ago,
are being revealed to us day by day.
God is merciful and gracious,
slow to anger and abounding in steadfast love.
God calls us to this time of worship
that we may know love that never gives up on us.
As the heavens are high above the earth,
so great is God's steadfast love.

INVOCATION

Open our mouths to sing your praise, O God, and turn us from the gods
we create. Renew our youth like the eagles, so we may soar to new
heights of faithfulness. Write your purposes on our hearts in this hour,
that a week amid the world's distractions may not erase our awareness of
your loving care for all people. Amen.

CALL TO CONFESSION

Come, all who have followed after false gods. Come, all who have sought
to reduce the one true God to codes and platitudes. Come, all who are
dissatisfied with the old wineskins. Come, all who know your inner need
for forgiveness and renewal. Let us confess the sin that separates us from
the wholeness God offers in Christ.

PRAYER OF CONFESSION

Holy God, how far we have wandered from your steadfast love and mercy!
We have allowed possessions to blind us to values, choosing illusions of
success over faithful service. In our prayers we have come asking you to
patch the old garments we are unwilling to give up. O God, we are lost.
Strip away all the sin that weighs us down. Grant us your mercy, and
clothe us anew with righteousness and justice. Through Christ. Amen.

ASSURANCE OF FORGIVENESS

God does not deal with us according to our sins, or repay us according to our iniquities. As far as the east is from the west, so far does God remove our transgressions from us. God redeems our lives from the pit and crowns us with steadfast love and mercy. Praise God! We are forgiven! The covenant is renewed! The Spirit gives new life! Amen.

COLLECT

In Christ we have confidence, O God, that you still speak in ways we can understand. Open before us now a door of hope, that we may be satisfied with good as long as we live. Write your word on our hearts and renew our confidence, that we may be ministers of your new covenant. Amen.

OFFERTORY INVITATION

Do not forget the benefits that God pours out on us day by day: air, light, water, food, and places of safety. Blessed with the abundance of God's mercy, let us demonstrate our thankfulness with generous support for the ministries of the church.

OFFERTORY PRAYER

We acknowledge your steadfast love, O Sovereign One, and commit ourselves anew to the just and caring use of the skills and resources you have granted us. Guide all the programs and outreach we undertake in the name of Christ. Amen.

COMMISSION AND BLESSING

When you enter the wilderness, God is there.
When hopes are shattered, the Eternal One cares.
  Through Christ we have confidence in God's love,
  and we face the world unafraid.
You are a letter from Jesus Christ,
to be written by God's Spirit on human hearts.
  We go forth as ministers of a new covenant,
  knowing that God gives us competence for the task.
You are carriers of God's steadfast love and mercy,
which you are called to share with others.
  We will serve in faithfulness,
  seeking to live God's justice and righteousness.
Amen.   **Amen.**

(See hymn No. 22.)

Last Sunday After Epiphany
(Transfiguration)

Old Testament: 2 Kings 2:1–12a
Psalm 50:1–6
Epistle: 2 Corinthians 4:3–6
Gospel: Mark 9:2–9

CALL TO WORSHIP

Come to the mountaintop to pray,
for God will not keep silence.
We gather to listen for God's word
and to make our response.
Come to the light of God's revelation,
for we are in darkness apart from God's love.
The light shines in our hearts, giving knowledge
of the glory of God in the face of Christ.
Come, as God's covenant people,
who serve and sacrifice in faithfulness.
The heavens declare God's righteousness
and draw us to the excitement of worship.

INVOCATION

Mighty God, beyond the whirlwind, fire, and tempest, speak to us as we worship and pray. Catch our attention, and keep our focus on the light you would bring us and on the people you want us to help. Open our eyes, our minds, and our hearts so we will be ready for your teaching and responsive to your life-changing purposes. Amen.

CALL TO CONFESSION

It is God who judges our faithfulness, and so it is to God that we bring our minds and hearts that have, too often, been blinded by the gods of this world. Let us confess our failures and our need.

PRAYER OF CONFESSION

O Sovereign God, we confess that we have allowed so many things to come between us and the gospel, that we cannot see the light of Christ or hear your voice calling us to listen. We have neither the courage nor the faith to respond effectively to your call. We are more concerned for our own safety and comfort than for the triumph of truth. As you forgive us again, we pray that you will lift the veil that blinds us. Save us from perishing, for the sake of Jesus Christ. Amen.

ASSURANCE OF FORGIVENESS

The heavens declare God's righteousness, and earth knows the generosity of our Creator. Christ has come in the likeness of God to set us free from our sin and to proclaim our wholeness. Know this day the glory of God in the face of Christ—and live! Amen.

COLLECT

In the glistening brightness of your presence we turn our attention to your teaching, fully attuned to what you want to say to us. May the light of the gospel so illuminate us that we receive a double portion of the prophet's spirit and the assurance that we are your beloved servants. For Christ's sake. Amen.

OFFERTORY INVITATION

Elijah used God's gifts to part the waters; may we at least use God's gifts to provide access to fresh water for those who have none. The disciples knew God's presence in the brightness, clouds, and voice on the mountaintop; may our offerings help provide the spiritual blessings God intends for us and all people. Let us give generously.

OFFERTORY PRAYER

Bless these offerings, O God, that they may alleviate human suffering and fears, lead us to the fullness of life Christ offers, and minister to the needs of people we will never know. May others see the glory of Christ because of our caring and sharing. Amen.

COMMISSION AND BLESSING

The voice of God, which called us to the mountaintop,
sends us back into our everyday world.
We scatter with God's word in our hearts
and the assurance of God's power sustaining us.
Take with you the light of God's revelation
and the knowledge of God's glory in Christ.
We seek to attune our spirits to our Creator,
that the light may shine for others through us.
Live in covenant with God and all God's people,
and your lives will be richly blessed.
We give ourselves, without counting the cost,
that the gospel may be proclaimed as we serve.
Amen.　　**Amen.**

(See hymn No. 23.)

The Season of Lent

Ash Wednesday

Old Testament: Joel 2:1–2, 12–17a
Psalm 51:1–12
Epistle: 2 Corinthians 5:20b—6:2 (3–10)
Gospel: Matthew 6:1–6, 16–21

CALL TO WORSHIP

Behold, now is the acceptable time.
Today is the day of God's salvation.
We tremble in fear and anticipation
at the nearness of a God so great and powerful.
Return with all your heart,
with weeping, fasting, and mourning.
God is gracious and merciful,
slow to anger and abounding in steadfast love.
Be reconciled to God, through Christ Jesus,
and receive a new and right spirit within.
We will fast and pray as an inner discipline,
preparing ourselves for faithful discipleship.

INVOCATION

We return to you, O God, in this solemn assembly of elders and children,
women and men, clergy and laity, asking you to bless us in this lenten
season and spare all your people. Lead us in the way of truth to the joy of
your salvation, and uphold us with willing spirits. Amen.

CALL TO CONFESSION

With trembling hearts, knowing that we seldom discern our own errors,
we turn ourselves toward the Eternal One. Now is the acceptable time;
now is the day of salvation. Come to the One who takes no delight in
burnt offerings, but accepts the sincere prayers of the penitent. Let us
repent and believe.

PRAYER OF CONFESSION

We come to you, O God, an unfaithful people. We have sinned against
you and done much that is evil in your sight. The shadows of sin dominate
us, and our secret faults separate us from the light and knowledge of your
presence. Have mercy on us, blot out our transgressions, forgive our
iniquity, and remember our sin no more. Purge us and we will be clean,
wash us and we will be purer than newfallen snow. Grant us, O God, a
new and right Spirit. Amen.

ASSURANCE OF FORGIVENESS

Jesus Christ, the source of our salvation, died for our sins, once for all, to put to death the trespasses in which we have been living and destroy the domination of evil among us. We have been reconciled to God, through Christ, and made partners in a new covenant. God is compassionate and merciful, granting us clean hearts and new life in Christ. Rejoice, open your lips, and let your mouths show forth the Creator's praise. Amen.

COLLECT

Share with us your promises and your prescriptions, Merciful God, for we need both the reassurance of your steadfast love and your call to responsible service. In this season we seek reconciliation and renewal. Establish in us those strengths of character that help us to withstand evil and endure hardships for the sake of the gospel. In you we live and rejoice and have everything we need. Speak to us now. Amen.

OFFERTORY INVITATION

Let us invest our treasures in the realm of the Sovereign One, seeking through these gifts to do God's will on earth. May we give, not so much from a sense of duty, as in celebration of the privilege of sharing.

OFFERTORY PRAYER

Thank you, God, for the joy of giving. It feels good to invest in the program and outreach of the church. We ask that many will come to know the richness of your grace through these gifts. Continue, we pray, your re-creative work in our midst and among the least and the greatest of our sisters and brothers. In Jesus' name. Amen.

COMMISSION AND BLESSING

Go forward with assurance and trust,
for God upholds and strengthens our spirits.
   We believe God knows and responds to our need,
   equipping us to endure and to grow.
Take with you the tools of righteousness,
genuine love and truthful speech.
   In honor or dishonor, good or ill repute,
   we will not waver from our intent to serve God.
The Eternal One is gracious and merciful,
slow to anger, and abounding in steadfast love.
   Our lenten fast will be with and for God alone,
   as we rend our hearts, not our garments.
Amen.   **Amen.**

(See hymns No. 24 and No. 25.)

First Sunday of Lent

Old Testament: Genesis 9:8–17
Psalm 25:1–10
Epistle: 1 Peter 3:18–22
Gospel: Mark 1:9–15

CALL TO WORSHIP

Lift up your souls to the Living God,
who enters into covenant with us.
We wait on our Maker, trusting God's kindness
and seeking to know God's ways.
Raise your eyes to behold the risen Christ,
who triumphs over death and destruction.
In Jesus Christ we renew our commitment
to share the good news of God's realm.
Attune yourselves to the Holy Spirit's gifts
and leave behind the wilderness of despair.
The Spirit sets us free from limits of the flesh,
from bondage to sin and decay.

INVOCATION

God of saving acts in human history, and lively promises for future fulfillment, equip us in this hour of worship to live fully in the present. Make your ways known to us and teach us your truth. Lead your humble servants in the way you would have us go. Be patient with us, we pray, for we are trying to be faithful. Amen.

CALL TO CONFESSION

With trembling hearts, knowing that we seldom discern our own errors, we turn ourselves toward the Eternal One. Now is the acceptable time; now is the day of salvation. Come to the One who takes no delight in burnt offerings, but accepts the sincere prayers of the penitent. Let us repent and believe.

PRAYER OF CONFESSION

We come to you, O God, an unfaithful people. We have sinned against you and done much that is evil in your sight. The shadows of sin dominate us, and our secret faults separate us from the light and knowledge of your presence. Have mercy on us, blot out our transgressions, forgive our iniquity, and remember our sin no more. Purge us and we will be clean, wash us and we will be purer than newfallen snow. Grant us, O God, a new and right Spirit. Amen.

ASSURANCE OF FORGIVENESS

Jesus Christ, the source of our salvation, died for our sins, once for all, to put to death the trespasses in which we have been living and destroy the domination of evil among us. We have been reconciled to God, through Christ, and made partners in a new covenant. God is compassionate and merciful, granting us clean hearts and new life in Christ. Rejoice, open your lips, and let your mouths show forth the Creator's praise. Amen.

COLLECT

In the covenant of baptism you have cleansed us. In Christ you have lifted us above the powers and authorities of this world to higher loyalties. Make plain to us now, O God, what you expect of us. Clear our consciences and fill our lives with new purpose. We pray in Jesus' name. Amen.

OFFERTORY INVITATION

In this season of sacrifice we are invited to reexamine our use of all the resources and abilities God allows us to manage here on earth. For reasons unknown to us we have been entrusted with almost limitless opportunities and obligations. Does our offering today give full expression to our faith, and God's faithfulness?

OFFERTORY PRAYER

We remember your steadfast love and mercy, which have removed our shame and drawn us into covenant with you, O God. Through these offerings we give thanks for your patience and loving-kindness. Direct these gifts toward the realization of your purposes for us. In Jesus' name. Amen.

COMMISSION AND BLESSING

Go forth to live as covenant people this week,
for God is everywhere present and available.
We would be led in God's ways,
devoting ourselves to self-examination and growth.
Reenter the everyday world, where Jesus walked,
learning from the example lived among us.
We dare to walk in the power of Christ's resurrection,
claiming our baptism as God's beloved children.
Rejoice in the Spirit's empowering gifts,
for God will enable your ministry.
Thanks be to God for opportunities
to make a difference in the world!
Amen.   **Amen.**

(See hymns No. 26 and No. 27.)

Second Sunday of Lent

Old Testament: Genesis 17:1–10, 15–19
Psalm 105:1–11
Epistle: Romans 4:16–25
Gospel: Mark 8:31–38
(Alternate) Mark 9:1–9

2/28/88

CALL TO WORSHIP

The way of worship invites us:
"Give thanks, call on God's name."
We remember God's wonderful works
and our hearts rejoice in God's presence.
The way of the covenant beckons us:
"Walk blameless before your God."
God awakens our faith and trust
and calls forth righteousness.
The way of the cross summons us:
"Deny yourself and follow."
Christ challenges our complacency
and bids us risk all for the gospel.

INVOCATION

God of Wonderful Deeds, we call on your name as we bring our words and works before you, seeking your affirmation and blessing. We are fully convinced that you are able to do according to your promises, and we want to live in covenant with you as disciples of Jesus Christ. Help us in this hour to break down the barriers that separate us from our highest intent. Amen.

CALL TO CONFESSION

With trembling hearts, knowing that we seldom discern our own errors, we turn ourselves toward the Eternal One. Now is the acceptable time; now is the day of salvation. Come to the One who takes no delight in burnt offerings, but accepts the sincere prayers of the penitent. Let us repent and believe.

PRAYER OF CONFESSION

We come to you, O God, an unfaithful people. We have sinned against you and done much that is evil in your sight. The shadows of sin dominate us, and our secret faults separate us from the light and knowledge of your presence. Have mercy on us, blot out our transgressions, forgive our iniquity, and remember our sin no more. Purge us and we will be clean, wash us and we will be purer than newfallen snow. Grant us, O God, a new and right Spirit. Amen.

ASSURANCE OF FORGIVENESS

Jesus Christ, the source of our salvation, died for our sins, once for all, to put to death the trespasses in which we have been living and destroy the domination of evil among us. We have been reconciled to God, through Christ, and made partners in a new covenant. God is compassionate and merciful, granting us clean hearts and new life in Christ. Rejoice, open your lips, and let your mouths show forth the Creator's praise. Amen.

COLLECT

In your wonderful works, O God, we rejoice. In your promises we have hope. By your grace we receive new life, even as we deny ourselves, take up Christ's cross, and follow. Our hearts rejoice, as your word instructs us anew. Amen.

OFFERTORY INVITATION

Jesus Christ risked all, that we might know the power of love. Let us give now, with that same abandon, to proclaim God's wonderful works, in Christ, to the whole world.

OFFERTORY PRAYER

May our offerings prove that we are neither ashamed of the gospel nor unwilling to risk all your gifts to us. We rejoice in your promises, O God, even as we give ourselves to serve in Christ's name. Use these gifts and our lives to bring your love to all humankind. Amen.

COMMISSION AND BLESSING

As we have met God in worship,
we go forth to encounter God in our work.
> **We depart as a covenant people**
> **whose highest loyalty is to Almighty God.**
The cross of Christ goes before us into the world,
reminding us of the cost of discipleship.
> **We face the realities of everyday life,**
> **intending to put God's purposes before our own gain.**
The promise and presence of God's covenant
go with us to strengthen our resolve.
> **Our hearts rejoice in God's wonderful works;**
> **we will praise God in our words and deeds.**
Amen.   **Amen.**

(See hymn No. 28.)

Third Sunday of Lent

Old Testament: Exodus 20:1–17
Psalm 19:7–14
Epistle: 1 Corinthians 1:22–25
Gospel: John 2:13–22

CALL TO WORSHIP

Gather to ponder the wisdom and law of God.
Draw near to share in God's strength and power.
The law of God is perfect, reviving the soul;
God's testimony is sure, making wise the simple.
The precepts of God are right, rejoicing the heart;
God's commandments are pure, enlightening the eyes.
The fear of God is clean, enduring forever;
God's ordinances are true and righteous altogether.
ALL: **Let the words of our mouths**
and the meditations of our hearts
be acceptable in your sight,
O God, our Rock and our Redeemer.

INVOCATION

O God, we come to your holy temple, not for what we can gain, but to
honor your name, not that others may think well of us, but that we may
pour out our thanksgiving. May we desire your truth more than gold,
your word more than the sweetness of honey, the power of your commandments beyond all our excuses. Alert us to your presence and make
yourself known to us in ways we cannot mistake. In Jesus' name. Amen.

CALL TO CONFESSION

With trembling hearts, knowing that we seldom discern our own errors,
we turn ourselves toward the Eternal One. Now is the acceptable time;
now is the day of salvation. Come to the One who takes no delight in
burnt offerings, but accepts the sincere prayers of the penitent. Let us
repent and believe.

PRAYER OF CONFESSION

3/7/94

We come to you, O God, an unfaithful people. We have sinned against
you and done much that is evil in your sight. The shadows of sin dominate
us, and our secret faults separate us from the light and knowledge of your
presence. Have mercy on us, blot out our transgressions, forgive our
iniquity, and remember our sin no more. Purge us and we will be clean,
wash us and we will be purer than newfallen snow. Grant us, O God, a
new and right Spirit. Amen.

ASSURANCE OF FORGIVENESS

Jesus Christ, the source of our salvation, died for our sins, once for all, to put to death the trespasses in which we have been living and destroy the domination of evil among us. We have been reconciled to God, through Christ, and made partners in a new covenant. God is compassionate and merciful, granting us clean hearts and new life in Christ. Rejoice, open your lips, and let your mouths show forth the Creator's praise. Amen.

COLLECT

Open to us your perfect law, O God, that we may live by its spirit of love. Empower us to embrace your foolishness rather than human wisdom, your weakness rather than human strength, the crucified and risen Christ rather than earthly principalities and powers. Help us to discern the errors within and among us that separate us from others, our own best selves, and you, as we listen to your holy word. Amen.

OFFERTORY INVITATION

The law of God challenges our priorities and turns us away from self-centered values. When we rate things above relationships and seek riches more than righteousness, we are confronted by eternal truths that call us once more to share and sacrifice. We bring our offerings as symbols of our self-dedication.

OFFERTORY PRAYER

As we honor you with these gifts, O God, we give thanks for all your blessings and pray that you will help us to be good stewards. Keep us from trading on your generosity for our own benefit rather than participating fully in your caring love for all humanity. May we be disciples and servants, not self-seeking money changers. In Jesus' name. Amen.

COMMISSION AND BLESSING

Go forth in the joy of serving God
and keeping God's commands and ordinances.
God's ways are not burdensome,
and God's wisdom, in Christ, empowers us.
Leave behind the dominion of presumptuous sins
and the tyranny of self-centered striving.
God cleanses us from our hidden faults
and grants us strength, not of this world.
Receive God's wisdom and strength
to guide all your thoughts and actions.
We receive anew God's perfect law of love,
with rejoicing hearts and enlightened eyes.
Amen.   **Amen.**

(See hymn No. 29.)

Fourth Sunday of Lent

Old Testament: Judges 4:4–9 (alt.)
2 Chronicles 36:14–23
Psalm 137:1–6
Epistle: Ephesians 2:4–10
Gospel: John 3:14–21

CALL TO WORSHIP

Come from your exile
to meet the God who sets us free.
What does it mean to be free?
How can we make the choices freedom offers?
Come from lives of unfaithfulness
to encounter the God whose care is unceasing.
What does faithfulness require of us?
How can we, unworthy ones, accept God's care?
Come from the shadows where you have hidden
to rejoice in the God who brings light and hope.
What will happen when our deeds are revealed?
How will our lives be changed by God's truth?

INVOCATION

O God, whose truth extends beyond the range of our questions, and
whose mercy reaches farther than our gravest sin, hear today the cries of
your people. Have compassion on us and meet us here, lest we be led
astray by our own schemes and the false gods we create. Reveal to us once
more the light you sent in Jesus, that it may illuminate our earthly
journey and help us to see and appreciate the life you intend for us.
Amen.

CALL TO CONFESSION

With trembling hearts, knowing that we seldom discern our own errors,
we turn ourselves toward the Eternal One. Now is the acceptable time;
now is the day of salvation. Come to the One who takes no delight in
burnt offerings, but accepts the sincere prayers of the penitent. Let us
repent and believe.

PRAYER OF CONFESSION

We come to you, O God, an unfaithful people. We have sinned against
you and done much that is evil in your sight. The shadows of sin dominate
us, and our secret faults separate us from the light and knowledge of your
presence. Have mercy on us, blot out our transgressions, forgive our
iniquity, and remember our sin no more. Purge us and we will be clean,

wash us and we will be purer than newfallen snow. Grant us, O God, a new and right Spirit. Amen.

ASSURANCE OF FORGIVENESS

Jesus Christ, the source of our salvation, died for our sins, once for all, to put to death the trespasses in which we have been living and destroy the domination of evil among us. We have been reconciled to God, through Christ, and made partners in a new covenant. God is compassionate and merciful, granting us clean hearts and new life in Christ. Rejoice, open your lips, and let your mouths show forth the Creator's praise. Amen.

COLLECT

May your word reassure us, O God. When we are afraid to face detractors and enemies, when we are so isolated that even you seem far away, when judgment comes and we are reluctant to face all that your light reveals. In your rich mercy lead us to times of singing and rejoicing, in spite of oppression, shadow, and separation. In the name of Jesus, who fully embodied your intent for humankind. Amen.

OFFERTORY INVITATION

In gratitude for God's light and mercy, in thanksgiving for the love that will not let us go, in joyful acknowledgment of the faith that binds us to one another and to our God, let us bring our offerings.

OFFERTORY PRAYER

We bring our treasure, O God, not to build monuments to ourselves, but to send messengers of your good news to all the world. We dedicate these gifts, not so much to enhance the programs and ministries of this congregation as for the sheer joy of proclaiming your goodness among all people. May our gifts reflect the depths of love we have known, and that we want to share. Amen.

COMMISSION AND BLESSING

Go forth in freedom,
to make the choices of another week.
We rejoice in the promise of God's mercy
and the assurance of God's guidance.
Go forth in faithfulness,
knowing God will not leave or forsake you.
We give thanks for God's steadfast love
and the saving grace of Jesus Christ.
Go forth in light,
seeking God's truth in all circumstances.
We celebrate the gospel's transforming power
and the brightness of God's new day.
Amen.   **Amen.**

(See hymn No. 30.)

Fifth Sunday of Lent

Old Testament: Jeremiah 31:31–34
Psalm 51:10–17
Epistle: Hebrews 5:7–10
Gospel: John 12:20–33

3/20/88

CALL TO WORSHIP

We have come for this hour to glorify God,
to sing the praises of the Most High.
We gather for the cleansing of our hearts
and the awakening of our spirits.
May God write the law of love on our hearts
and restore in us the joy of salvation.
We seek deliverance from temptation and guilt,
and forgiveness for all our sin.
Let us enter into covenant obedience,
even if faithfulness leads to a cross.
We want to lift up our voices
and renew our vows to be God's people.

INVOCATION

O God, whose love is over all the children of your grace and whose
judgment lifts up rather than destroys, hear our cries. Meet us now for
we would see Jesus and, through that obedient life, know you. Restore us
to a covenant relationship in which we can find the fullness of life you
intend, and offer it to a needy world. Amen.

CALL TO CONFESSION

With trembling hearts, knowing that we seldom discern our own errors,
we turn ourselves toward the Eternal One. Now is the acceptable time;
now is the day of salvation. Come to the One who takes no delight in
burnt offerings, but accepts the sincere prayers of the penitent. Let us
repent and believe.

PRAYER OF CONFESSION

We come to you, O God, ~~and~~ as an unfaithful people. We have sinned against
you and done much that is evil in your sight. The shadows of sin dominate
us, and our secret faults separate us from the light and knowledge of your
presence. Have mercy on us, blot out our transgressions, forgive our
iniquity, and remember our sin no more. Purge us and we will be clean,
wash us and we will be purer than newfallen snow. Grant us, O God, a
new and right Spirit, ~~Amen.~~ for we pray in the name of
Jesus our Lord, who comes to us as your Christ, Amen.

ASSURANCE OF FORGIVENESS

Jesus Christ, the source of our salvation, died for our sins, once for all, to put to death the trespasses in which we have been living and destroy the domination of evil among us. We have been reconciled to God, through Christ, and made partners in a new covenant. God is compassionate and merciful, granting us clean hearts and new life in Christ. Rejoice, open your lips, and let your mouths show forth the Creator's praise. Amen.

COLLECT

Reveal your presence and your purposes, suffering God, that we may have the courage to face life and death with joy. May your word heal our broken spirits and contrite hearts, empowering us to follow Jesus and live as your servant people. Speak now to our troubled souls through your living word. Amen.

OFFERTORY INVITATION

God takes no delight in burnt offerings or sacrifices that we bring apart from the commitment of ourselves. Let us not seek to hoard our lives and possessions as if they belonged to us, but rather glorify God with our generosity.

OFFERTORY PRAYER

Our hearts would not withhold our devotion, or our hands grasp for ourselves what you summon us to give. May these gifts signify our commitment to follow Jesus. Receive these offerings and instruct us in their use, to your honor and glory. Amen.

COMMISSION AND BLESSING

A new day is dawning when God's promises
will be renewed in the risen Christ.
All of us will know God,
from the least of us to the greatest.
We are people of the covenant,
in touch with the Eternal in our midst.
God has acted in Christ to save us,
that we might live as children of God.
Go forth as followers and servants,
among all who are being drawn to Christ.
We take the risks of faith,
rejoicing in our discipleship.
Amen.   **Amen.**

(See hymn No. 31.)

Sixth Sunday of Lent
(Palm Sunday)

Old Testament: Isaiah 50:4–9a
Psalm 118:19–29
Epistle: Philippians 2:5–11
Gospel: Mark 11:1–11

CALL TO WORSHIP

God wakens us to this new day
and bids us enter the gates of righteousness.
This is the day that God has made.
We will rejoice and be glad in it.
The stone that the builders rejected
has become the cornerstone of our faith.
This is God's doing;
it is marvelous in our eyes.
God causes light to shine on us
and blesses our festive procession.
Blessed is the One who comes in God's name.
Hosanna in the highest!

INVOCATION

We give thanks, God of all seasons, for this time of heightened emotions
and anticipation. In the midst of frightening circumstances we look to the
calm, steady, humble One, who is still alive in our midst. We invoke the
name of Jesus Christ on behalf of all who celebrate and all who pass by
unseeing. Bless us all for Christ's sake, and for our growth in faith. Amen.

CALL TO CONFESSION

We stand together in our need for forgiveness. Something of each of us is
recognizable in the Palm Sunday crowds who greeted Jesus en route to
the temple. We share their shortsightedness and their sin. Let us turn
away from all that separates us from God's purposes, as we unite in
prayer.

PRAYER OF CONFESSION

Sovereign God, we come confessing our guilt and seeking to be free from
our willful self-centered ways. False pride cuts us off from other people
and dims our eyes and ears to your way. We turn from your Chosen One,
for Jesus' example is too demanding, and we are unprepared to accept the
horrible death on a cross as a sacrifice for us. Who will vindicate us before
you, as we seek change within? Hear us, O God! Amen.

ASSURANCE OF FORGIVENESS

God hears our prayers and helps us. God lifts from us the burden of our guilt and offers us the mind of Christ. In our newfound humility we are granted strength not known before. In obedience to God we find true freedom. Now we can shout our hosannas with real enthusiasm. We have good news to celebrate! We are forgiven! Amen.

COLLECT

The day is yours, O God, and we rejoice that you have awakened us to share in it. As we hear again the phrases and stories so familiar to us, help us to identify ourselves in the words and actions of people long ago. So touch us that our lives may reflect your teaching, join your parade, and bow down before your glory. Amen.

OFFERTORY INVITATION

God does not take our possessions, unbidden, to use for the world's needy, but God does invite our sharing. Many risked much on the first Palm Sunday—their wardrobes, their reputations, their lives. What, for us, represents fitting participation in God's parade? God welcomes whatever you are ready to give.

OFFERTORY PRAYER

If we had a donkey to lend to Jesus, we would do so. If we could ease Christ's way to Calvary, or prevent its cruelty, we would act. But these are not ours to give. So we offer what we have: the tithes and offerings we have brought for your blessing—and all the riches we retain for ourselves. Use everything we are and have to advance Christ's reign among us. Amen.

COMMISSION AND BLESSING

God sends us forth, each with our own mission,
to hasten the day of Christ's rule.
**We are ready to serve where God sends us,
and to do what God requires.**
This is a day God has made;
let us continue to rejoice and be glad in it.
**God has opened to us the gates of righteousness.
We will go through them with joy.**
God has caused light to shine on us
and offered salvation to transform us.
**We give thanks for the goodness of God
whose steadfast love endures forever.**
Amen. **Amen.**

(See hymn No. 32.)

Sixth Sunday of Lent
(Passion Sunday)

Old Testament: Isaiah 50:4–9a
Psalm 31:9–16
Epistle: Philippians 2:5–11
Gospel: Mark 14—15 or 15:1–39

CALL TO WORSHIP
Our times are in God's hands;
let us worship in confidence and trust.
God awakens our ears and our tongues
to hear and answer God's call.
When distress and grief weigh us down,
God's steadfast love is present with us.
God comes to us in our sorrow and pain,
bringing new strength and hope.
When we are tempted to deny and betray,
God does not forsake us.
God is here, and we are drawn to worship.
God is with us; we will not fear.

INVOCATION
Faithful God, we stand together, saints and sinners, seeking your deliverance. Let your face shine on your servants, and save us with your steadfast love. Teach us to trust you, and help us to be worthy of one another's trust. In Jesus' name. Amen.

CALL TO CONFESSION
The march of events during Holy Week troubles us, for the tragedy seems to be repeated down to our own day. Goodness is envied and rejected by the impatient and the self-satisfied. We find ourselves in their company, despite our best intentions. Let us confess our sin.

PRAYER OF CONFESSION
All you have taught us, O God, we have forgotten or ignored in our weariness and distress. The cross has become for us a stumbling block and folly. In shame and confusion we have perpetrated injustice rather than fighting it, and hidden in the shadows rather than carrying the light of your truth into the world. Call us back into covenant, we pray, forgiving our grievous sin and reclaiming us from our dead works to a living hope. May others see Jesus through our faithful and selfless service. Amen.

ASSURANCE OF FORGIVENESS

Listen! God has called us in righteousness and delivers us from our shame. God comforts and protects. We can lean on God in hope and trust, for God is healing and freeing us to walk in the light and become lights to others. Praise God! Amen.

COLLECT

Teach us, Gracious God, to know the mind of Christ and live by his example of humble obedience. Meet us in the midst of our brokenness and unfaithfulness, to heal and restore. Let your face shine on us, even in the shadow of the cross, where we feel alone and forsaken. We entrust our times to your unfailing hands. Amen.

OFFERTORY INVITATION

Before the One who poured out life itself on our behalf, we pause in awe and wonder. The costliest gifts we might pour out today could not match Christ's sacrifices for us. May we give in grateful thanksgiving and humble commitment.

OFFERTORY PRAYER

Thank you, God, for your saving action in Jesus Christ, and for the opportunity to join in the tasks of ministry you set before us. May our offerings fulfill your purposes and never betray your trust. In Jesus' name. Amen.

COMMISSION AND BLESSING

Carry with you into the world the mind of Christ,
who forsook equality with God in humble obedience.
In self-emptying love Christ became a servant
so we might know God's glory.
Face your own suffering in the shadow of the cross,
knowing that Christ shares your pain.
In grateful trust we seek to serve,
passing on the good news we've been taught.
God's face shines on you, with steadfast love,
equipping you for each day's need.
Our times are in God's hands!
We will not fear, even when our strength fails.
Amen.   **Amen.**

(See hymn No. 33.)

Monday of Holy Week

Old Testament: Isaiah 42:1–9
Psalm 36:5–10
Epistle: Hebrews 9:11–15
Gospel: John 12:1–11

CALL TO WORSHIP

Come to the high mountains of God's righteousness;
know also the depths of God's judgments.
We feast on the abundance of God's house
and drink from the rivers of God's delights.
Come to the fountain of life
and to the light of God's steadfast love.
We give thanks for God's covenant in Christ
and seek to be carriers of truth and hope.
Give ear to God's call to justice for all
and share in the new things God declares.
We rejoice in the redemption Christ brings
and welcome the promised eternal inheritance.

INVOCATION

Creator of All Worlds, who stretched forth the heavens and encircled
them with your steadfast love, surround us here with evidence of your
saving power and your concern for each one of us. You have given us
breath and spirit; grant us now your light that we may see more clearly
and follow more faithfully. In Jesus' name. Amen.

CALL TO CONFESSION

The march of events during Holy Week troubles us, for the tragedy seems
to be repeated down to our own day. Goodness is envied and rejected by
the impatient and the self-satisfied. We find ourselves in their company,
despite our best intentions. Let us confess our sin.

PRAYER OF CONFESSION

All you have taught us, O God, we have forgotten or ignored in our
weariness and distress. The cross has become for us a stumbling block
and folly. In shame and confusion we have perpetrated injustice rather
than fighting it, and hidden in the shadows rather than carrying the light
of your truth into the world. Call us back into covenant, we pray, forgiving
our grievous sin and reclaiming us from our dead works to a living hope.
May others see Jesus through our faithful and selfless service. Amen.

ASSURANCE OF FORGIVENESS

Listen! God has called us in righteousness and delivers us from our shame. God comforts and protects. We can lean on God in hope and trust, for God is healing and freeing us to walk in the light and become lights to others. Praise God! Amen.

COLLECT

We, who often join the crowds to view spectacular events, gather now as if in small groups at our Savior's feet. By the sacrifices of Christ our consciences are being purified and we are moving from dead works to serve the living God. Inspire us now to identify with Christ's mission to bring wholeness and true freedom to all your children. Amen.

OFFERTORY INVITATION

With the example of Mary before us may we, too, give of our best to proclaim our love for Jesus Christ. May nothing we devote to this house of prayer be wasted, and may true concern for the poor, the suffering, and the imprisoned move us to generous sharing. Amen.

OFFERTORY PRAYER

As we feast on the abundance you provide during this holy week, we would sacrifice to bring your justice to all nations and all peoples. Keep us from tokenism and merely going through the motions of faith. Touch our deepest emotions and transform our actions, that we may live among others the steadfast love you intend for all. To that end, bless and multiply this offering. Amen.

COMMISSION AND BLESSING

Reenter your everyday world as God's servants,
with courage, and commitment to justice.
   God takes us by the hand,
   that we might reach out to help others.
God offers light to disperse life's shadows,
and love to assuage our fears.
   God opens the eyes of the blind
   and brings prisoners from gloomy dungeons.
God's salvation is for the upright of heart,
and God's promises for all who accept the call.
   We receive Christ's commission with joy
   and go forth to be a blessing to others.
Amen.   **Amen.**

(See hymn No. 34.)

Tuesday of Holy Week

Old Testament: Isaiah 49:1–7
Psalm 71:1–12
Epistle: 1 Corinthians 1:18–31
Gospel: John 12:20–36

CALL TO WORSHIP

What brings us to this time of worship?
Why are we here today?
We wish to see Jesus,
the One who sacrificed life for us.
How far are we willing to go?
Dare we follow wherever truth leads?
We love the life God has granted us,
but it has no meaning apart from Christ.
Are we ready to leave the shadows of comfort
for the risks of discipleship?
Our souls are troubled away from God's light,
and we long for life with eternity in it.

INVOCATION

Meet us here, God of All Creation, to turn our values right side up. We have subscribed to the world's wisdom for too long and chased after goals that do not satisfy. Now we hear your voice summoning us to your light. We are ready to praise you and be guided by your word. Show us your way. Amen.

CALL TO CONFESSION

The march of events during Holy Week troubles us, for the tragedy seems to be repeated down to our own day. Goodness is envied and rejected by the impatient and the self-satisfied. We find ourselves in their company, despite our best intentions. Let us confess our sin.

PRAYER OF CONFESSION

All you have taught us, O God, we have forgotten or ignored in our weariness and distress. The cross has become for us a stumbling block and folly. In shame and confusion we have perpetrated injustice rather than fighting it, and hidden in the shadows rather than carrying the light of your truth into the world. Call us back into covenant, we pray, forgiving our grievous sin and reclaiming us from our dead works to a living hope. May others see Jesus through our faithful and selfless service. Amen.

ASSURANCE OF FORGIVENESS

Listen! God has called us in righteousness and delivers us from our shame. God comforts and protects. We can lean on God in hope and trust, for God is healing and freeing us to walk in the light and become lights to others. Praise God! Amen.

COLLECT

O God, who called us from the womb and blessed us in our parents' arms, speak our names again as prophets and evangelists declare your saving activity for humankind. We have trusted, and you have not failed us, but we have reached for proofs and doubted your love. We have chased the world's foolishness while ignoring the wisdom of Christ. Enable us now to hear and act on your truth. Amen.

OFFERTORY INVITATION

What you plant will bear fruit. What you share will pass on God's gifts to others. Answer God's call with your whole being as you offer material sacrifices for the work God summons us to do. Let us give as we have been blessed.

OFFERTORY PRAYER

We are in debt to you, God of All Creation, for the gift of life and for the Light by which we are being saved. There is no adequate response to your love except to share it. This we seek to do through our offerings of money, time, and devotion. Bless us in your service, we pray. Amen.

COMMISSION AND BLESSING

Have we encountered the One we sought
and found meaning and strength for our days?
  Christ, the power and wisdom of God,
  has found us and claimed us as disciples.
Will we go where we are sent
and respond where we are most needed?
  To walk in light, we must be children of light,
  in whom Christ is served as we follow Jesus.
Is our discipleship empowered by the cross
and guided by wisdom not our own?
  Christ is our wisdom, our righteousness,
  our sanctification, and our redemption.
Praise God!   **Amen.**

(See hymn No. 35.)

Wednesday of Holy Week

Old Testament: Isaiah 50:4–9a
Psalm 70
Epistle: Hebrews 12:1–3
Gospel: John 13:21–30

CALL TO WORSHIP

Surrounded by a cloud of witnesses,
we approach the God of grace and glory.
Laying aside every weight of sin and need,
we seek to run well the race of life.
Look to Jesus, life's pioneer and perfecter,
who endured even the cross with abiding joy.
The One who endured hostility from strangers
lifts us up when we are weary and fainthearted.
Seek here the blessing and forgiveness of God
amid the guilt and pain of misplaced loyalties.
Our God teaches, vindicates, and lifts us up
above the shame of hostility and betrayal.

INVOCATION

Deliver us, O God, from the worst in ourselves and from all who desire
our hurt. Out of the shame, confusion, and dishonor of our misdirected
lives, call us back to yourself and let us know your salvation. You are
great, O God, and greatly to be praised. Hasten to be with us, for we
need your help. Amen.

CALL TO CONFESSION

The march of events during Holy Week troubles us, for the tragedy seems
to be repeated down to our own day. Goodness is envied and rejected by
the impatient and the self-satisfied. We find ourselves in their company,
despite our best intentions. Let us confess our sin.

PRAYER OF CONFESSION

All you have taught us, O God, we have forgotten or ignored in our
weariness and distress. The cross has become for us a stumbling block
and folly. In shame and confusion we have perpetrated injustice rather
than fighting it, and hidden in the shadows rather than carrying the light
of your truth into the world. Call us back into covenant, we pray, forgiving
our grievous sin and reclaiming us from our dead works to a living hope.
May others see Jesus through our faithful and selfless service. Amen.

ASSURANCE OF FORGIVENESS

Listen! God has called us in righteousness and delivers us from our shame. God comforts and protects. We can lean on God in hope and trust, for God is healing and freeing us to walk in the light and become lights to others. Praise God! Amen.

COLLECT

Eternal Teacher, waken our ears to your word, through which you equip us to serve. Lead us once more to your Word-made-flesh, through whom our lives are freed from their burden of sin and guilt. May we together so embody your word that others will recognize Christ in us. Amen.

OFFERTORY INVITATION

In our poverty and spiritual need God has come to us in Christ with resources more generous than we can claim. Now our response may proclaim, "God is great!" Let us give our best as God has blessed us.

OFFERTORY PRAYER

Rejoicing in our salvation, we bring our offerings of thanksgiving and praise. As we have been taught, we would teach others through our time and gifts. As we have been forgiven and helped, we here offer the same to our sisters and brothers. Amen.

COMMISSION AND BLESSING

Join the cloud of witnesses who rejoice
in the salvation God offers in Christ.
We have good news to proclaim
in all the relationships of our lives.
Remember God's forgiveness of your sin
as you face those who have wronged you.
We have been freed to forgive others
as God, in Christ, has pardoned us.
Walk with Jesus through denial and betrayal,
as the cross looms large and Calvary draws near.
We rejoice in the opportunity to praise God
and honor our Savior this week.
Amen.   **Amen.**

(See hymn No. 36.)

Maundy Thursday

Old Testament: Exodus 24:3–8
Psalm 116:12–19
Epistle: 1 Corinthians 10:16–17
Gospel: Mark 14:12–26

CALL TO WORSHIP

Amid all good things competing for our attention,
where shall we go to find bread?
We come to the upper room,
seeking a table prepared for Jesus' disciples.
Among all the activities we can choose,
where shall we invest our time and efforts?
The church invites our discipleship,
calling us into the body of Christ.
Among all who claim our loyalty,
who encompasses the whole of life and truth?
God in Christ offers us wholeness,
bringing all the pieces of our lives together.

INVOCATION

On this holy night, filled with ominous foreboding, we dare to come to
the feast of life. We gather to honor Jesus, who showed us the way of
faithful service, and loved us enough to give up this earthly existence that
we might know your unconditional love. In thanksgiving and praise we
come to commune and find our identity with Christ. Amen.

CALL TO CONFESSION

The psalmist assures us that the death of the saints is precious in God's
sight. Tonight we have gathered in the shadow of Jesus' death for the sins
of all humankind. We have answered the invitation of a loving God who
wills that none of us be lost in our disobedience, self-centeredness, and
alienation. Let us pray that all our sin may be wiped away.

PRAYER OF CONFESSION

Merciful God, we are torn between the specter of Good Friday and the
feast Christ spreads before us. We come with the sorrowful question, "Is
it I?" We know the answer, for we have denied and betrayed. We have
broken covenant and turned from grace. We are ruled by what seems to
work at the moment, not by eternal verities. How can we ask for forgiveness when we find it so difficult to change? Good God, deliver us.
Loving Savior, grant pardon and transformation! Amen.

ASSURANCE OF FORGIVENESS

God offers us the cup of salvation, not as something we have earned, but as a gift to all who will accept it. The blood of the new covenant is poured out for many. Take and drink! Christ's body is broken for you. Take and eat! Know the costly, healing act by which you are set free from the burden of your sin and offered new life in Christ. Praise God! Amen.

COLLECT

God of All Generations, whose covenant with humankind, once sealed with the blood of sacrifices, was reaffirmed in the life and death of Jesus, we call on your name and seek your word. Take all our diversity, at this table spread around the world, and make us one body. Remove the evil that divides and immobilizes us, so we may know the power of your love at work in our midst. In Jesus' name. Amen.

OFFERTORY INVITATION

What shall we render to God for all God's bounty to us? Let us bring vows of faithfulness and offer sacrifices of thanksgiving. May our gifts be a worthy response to the greatest of all gifts—our salvation in Jesus Christ.

OFFERTORY PRAYER

We dedicate the work of our hands to building the community of saints. May our offerings be a hymn of praise to our Creator and a song of thanksgiving to our Redeemer. May they further Christ's mission and accomplish your will for humanity. Amen.

COMMISSION AND BLESSING

We have prayed and broken bread;
we have been forgiven and fed.
    Praise God for the bread of heaven
    and the cup of salvation.
Now we go out to face life's temptations and demands,
knowing we cannot stand alone against them.
    We are united with Christ and one another
    in a covenant that equips us for life.
God blesses us with gifts and freedom
and empowers our service.
    We go forth in confidence to face life's riches
    and undertake our servanthood.
Amen.   **Amen.**

(See hymn No. 37.)

Good Friday

Old Testament: Isaiah 52:13—53:12
Psalm 22:1–18
Epistle: Hebrews 4:14–16; 5:7–9
Gospel: John 18—19 or 19:17–30

CALL TO WORSHIP

We who have known failure and defeat
are summoned to walk with Jesus to Calvary.
   We who face weakness and temptation
   gather in the name of one who overcame them.
It is hard to recognize the bearer of sorrows
who was wounded for our transgressions.
   Yet we seek salvation in one despised and rejected,
   from whom there came no violence or deceit.
Let us come believing what we have heard
and acting on what has been revealed to us.
   We trust Christ to deliver and save us,
   to teach us obedience and faithfulness.
Amen.   **Amen.**

INVOCATION

When we feel alone and forgotten, we remember, O God, that your
Chosen One felt the depths of grief and despair. Despised, rejected, spat
upon, and scorned, Jesus continued to trust you and believe in the
mission you prescribed. As we gather to remember, we seek the faith that
triumphed over every adversity. Amen.

CALL TO CONFESSION

Come to the oppressed and afflicted One, who bears others' iniquities
and makes intercession for transgressors. Come to the Great High Priest,
who sympathizes with our weakness and leads us to the throne of grace.

PRAYER OF CONFESSION

In Christ's name we confess our plight, O God. We are poured out like
water and our strength is dried up. Like sheep, we have gone astray,
following our own whims and desires. We feel cut off from the land of the
living, for we have followed the dead-end paths of our own seeming self-
interest. Rescue us from our poor choices, or at least help us to bear their
consequences with the triumphant Spirit of Christ. Amen.

ASSURANCE OF FORGIVENESS

What we deserve, Christ has carried for us—the chastisement by which we are made whole, the stripes by which we are healed. Jesus has become the source of eternal salvation to all who obey. May the will of God prosper in us! Amen.

COLLECT

Lead us, Great God of the Universe, along the earthly paths toward Golgotha. From betrayal in the garden through trials, mocking, and torture, from the desertion of the disciples to the watch at the cross, we would see Jesus. As we suffer with Christ, strengthen us to face those calamities we must bear, with faithfulness to your will and trust in your purposes. Amen.

OFFERTORY INVITATION

God has not forsaken us in the worst of our troubles. Indeed, we have been richly blessed. We respond to God's generosity in our service through the church and in the offerings we bring to proclaim good news. May our deeds and our dollars reach out into our community and wherever our sisters and brothers are in need.

OFFERTORY PRAYER

God of Compassion and Love, bless our efforts and our offerings and multiply their effectiveness in proclaiming the reign of your truth among us. May your great act of giving inspire renewed commitment from all of us who wait here at the cross. Amen.

COMMISSION AND BLESSING

Carry with you the weight of Jesus' dying,
for there is no Easter apart from suffering.
**Christ was wounded for our transgressions
and bruised for our iniquities.**
What does Jesus' death mean for our own lives?
Are we freed from our bondage to sin?
**A weight has been lifted from us;
we can walk without fear in fullness of life.**
As our ancestors looked to God for deliverance,
we, too, trust God, even in this dark hour.
**From Jesus we have learned trust and obedience,
even in times of suffering and death.**
Amen.   **Amen.**

(See hymn No. 38.)

The Easter Season

Easter Sunday

Historic Message: Acts 10:34–43
Psalm 118:14–24
Epistle: 1 Corinthians 15:1–11
Gospel: John 20:1–18

CALL TO WORSHIP
God is acting in our midst
as we gather to celebrate good news.
This is the day that God has made;
let us rejoice and be glad in it.
Death has no claim
on those who live in Christ Jesus.
We shall not die, but we shall live
and recount the deeds of God.
By God's grace Christ died for our sins
and appears among us now to claim our loyalty.
Open the gates of righteousness that we may enter.
God has answered us in Christ, our salvation.

INVOCATION
God of Unexplained Mysteries and Unexpected Events, we rejoice in the good news of Easter. Good triumphs. There is healing salvation for all people of the earth. We have at hand a promise of peace the world cannot give. May the power of Christ's presence be so real to us here in worship that we are forever changed and made whole. Amen.

CALL TO CONFESSION
We who have doubted, rejected, and turned away are invited to express before God all that keeps us from claiming God's promises and living in peace with our sisters and brothers. Let us open our hearts to make room for the newness of life Christ offers.

PRAYER OF CONFESSION
Gracious God, in whom there is no partiality, we confess that our love is limited to those with whom we choose to associate. Our faith is restricted to what we can prove. Our service is reduced by our greater interest in the trappings of success. We have allowed religion to become a compartment in our lives, rather than leaven that influences and transforms the whole. O God, forgive our unfaithfulness and make today a time of new beginnings. In Jesus' name. Amen.

ASSURANCE OF FORGIVENESS

Jesus commanded us to preach and testify, to bear witness to forgiveness of sins. Christ died for our sins, according to the scriptures. Let us live, therefore, as forgiven and forgiving people. Amen.

COLLECT

As we listen for your word, call us by name, O God, as Jesus spoke to Mary in the garden. May the scriptures speak directly to our souls, moving us to a deeper relationship with you and fuller commitment to the work you call us to do. Roll away the stones that imprison our minds and hearts so we may know the healing touch of the risen Christ, in whose name we pray. Amen.

OFFERTORY INVITATION

The ministry and mission, death and resurrection of Jesus have become the cornerstone of our faith. Through our offerings we seek to enlarge God's building, that people of every nation may know they are accepted and loved. Let us give as God has blessed us.

OFFERTORY PRAYER

May these offerings bear witness to our faith in you and our confidence in your forgiving love for all humanity. Thank you for answering our prayers and providing for our salvation. With our gifts we hope to extend the good news of Easter beyond this community and this nation. Amen.

COMMISSION AND BLESSING

Take the good news of Easter
into your everyday world.
We have seen Jesus!
In Christ, life triumphs over death.
May this special day
make all your days special from now on.
All our days are God's gift to us;
we will rejoice and be glad in them.
The first disciples saw and believed;
let us, like them, carry the message to others.
By God's grace I am what I am,
and God's grace is not in vain.
Amen.   **Amen.**

(See hymns No. 39 and No. 40.)

Easter Sunday (Alternate Reading)

Old Testament: Isaiah 25:6–9
                    Psalm 118:14–24
Epistle: Acts 10:34–43
Gospel: Mark 16:1–8

CALL TO WORSHIP

Hear the amazing good news:
Jesus Christ is alive!
    Praise God, who has lifted the veil of death
    and wiped away our tears.
This is our God, for whom we have waited,
that we might be saved.
    Let us be glad and rejoice in God's salvation,
    and the good news of peace by Jesus Christ.
We are witnesses to the impact of Jesus' life
and the saving power of Jesus' sacrifice.
    This is the day that God has made;
    we will rejoice and be glad in it.

INVOCATION

Amazing and Surprising God, we come to this mountaintop day to be fed and freed. Show us our salvation in the depth of our beings so we can never again be the same. Roll away the stones that keep us from all that is true and right, that we might live without pretense or fear as followers of Jesus. Amen.

CALL TO CONFESSION

Bring your doubts and fears, your grief and pain, to these moments of prayer, as we seek forgiveness and healing. May all that we have sought to cover up and hide be exposed to God's saving, transforming presence. Face your own sin and give it to God as we pray in silence and together.

PRAYER OF CONFESSION

We tremble, Mighty God, before your awesome power to bring good from evil, new life from death. We have done things our own way, putting ourselves first and sometimes trying to be God. We have rejected the way of Jesus, whom you made faith's cornerstone, because self-giving love seems so impractical and dangerous. O God, we want to live more faithful lives, for our old behavior is unfulfilling, and there is no peace inside us or around us. Help us, God, and deliver us from our own evil. Amen.

ASSURANCE OF FORGIVENESS

God swallows up death, wipes away tears, and takes away our reproach. We shall not die, but live to recount the deeds of God. Let us be glad and rejoice in God's salvation, for it comes to each one who is open to receiving the gift. Praise God! Alleluia! Amen.

COLLECT

Open our eyes and ears to your marvelous involvement among us, Great God of the Universe, for you have visited our planet to show us the way you intend for us. We are here, not just as spectators, but to be witnesses to all Jesus said and did. Help us to hear the stories again, as if personally involved. Speak to each one in ways we can understand. Amen.

OFFERTORY INVITATION

We who feast on the mountaintop of God's blessing are called to share the feast with the world. We seek to do that through our own individual witness and through the programs and outreach of this church. It is a privilege to give of ourselves and our substance. Let us bring our offerings with joy.

OFFERTORY PRAYER

We rejoice in the privilege of sharing in your work among us, O God of Hosts. May these offerings witness to all Jesus said and did, both as we gather for inspiration and growth and as we extend helping hands around the world. Empower our lives to preach more powerfully than ever words could do, for we offer ourselves with our gifts. Amen.

COMMISSION AND BLESSING

We have visited the empty tomb
and heard again God's youthful messengers.
> **Do not be amazed; Jesus has risen.**
> **Return to your homes; Jesus will meet you there.**
We are witnesses to all Jesus did,
in Galilee, Judea, and Jerusalem.
> **Now Jesus works in our midst,**
> **and Christ lives through us today.**
As Jesus was anointed with the Holy Spirit's power,
for a ministry of healing and doing good,
> **We are commissioned for our ministry.**
> **God empowers us to "go and tell."**
Amen.   **Amen.**

(See hymn No. 41.)

Easter Evening

Historic Message: Acts 5:29–32 or Daniel 12:1–3
Psalm 150
Epistle: 1 Corinthians 5:6–8
Gospel: Luke 24:13–49

CALL TO WORSHIP

In our dim evenings, as in the bright dawns of life,
may we see and recognize our risen Savior.
We have walked with Christ and did not know it;
we have heard good news and did not claim it.
Come now to receive the gospel,
to embrace the story of Easter as your own.
Are the rumors really true?
Such strange events trouble and frighten us.
What we cannot explain proves true;
what we dare not hope has come to be.
Do not our hearts burn within us
as Jesus Christ becomes real to us on life's way?

INVOCATION

We come again, as doubters and believers, to meet Christ. Just when we think Jesus is too far from life's realities to understand, we find we are the ones who do not know what is going on. How can we comprehend Easter? Grant us true wisdom in this hour to discern Christ's presence and to awaken to your everlasting dawn. Through Christ. Amen.

CALL TO CONFESSION

On this day of celebration, when we focus on life and hope, we may not be ready for the good news unless we first remove the barriers to our receiving it. Bring now your fears and doubts, your broken relationships and failed promises. Confess all before God who hears and forgives.

PRAYER OF CONFESSION

All-powerful God, we are ashamed and penitent, for we have been obeying the forces of destruction rather than pursuing the good you intend. We cling to the old leaven of malice and evil, turning away from sincerity and truth. Forgive us, we pray, and turn us toward righteousness. In Jesus' name. Amen.

ASSURANCE OF FORGIVENESS

All who repent will know the forgiveness Christ brings. We are raised from the dust of our narrow perceptions and human schemes to share the light of God's eternity. Join with heaven and earth in a great song of praise to God, who grants life and wisdom so we may shine like the brightness of the firmament. Amen.

COLLECT

God of empty tombs and quiet talks, of unexplained visions and shared meals, confront us again in the mystery of Easter. Lift us out of our stale, unimaginative existence to join the chorus of exultation and praise that rises to witness to your saving love. Clothe us with power from on high, that we may turn many to righteousness. Amen.

OFFERTORY INVITATION

As our spiritual ancestors worshiped God with the sacrifice of their best animals, we bring our offerings and our high intentions to join the chorus of praise. God alone knows the depth of our commitment and the generosity of each gift. May our offerings be a worthy response to the blessings God has given.

OFFERTORY PRAYER

All praise to you, O God, for your mighty deeds. We join the chorus of trumpets, pipes, and strings to acknowledge your greatness. Receive these offerings of thanksgiving for raising Jesus Christ from the dead to be our salvation. Let all our gifts and our time give praise to your Holy Name. Amen.

COMMISSION AND BLESSING

Christ walks with us in newness of life;
go forth in confidence and joy!
> **We are the hands and feet of Jesus,**
> **carrying God's love and forgiveness to others.**
We are the only scriptures some will read.
Jesus will be known by our deeds.
> **In awe and obedience we accept our tasks,**
> **with humble sincerity and truth.**
Let everything that breathes praise God,
who equips us for our ministry.
> **We praise God, not with boasting or sham,**
> **but with honest delight in our mission, in Christ.**
Amen.   **Amen.**

(See hymns No. 42 and No. 43.)

Second Sunday of Easter

Historic Message: Acts 4:32–35
Psalm 133
Epistle: 1 John 1:1—2:2
Gospel: John 20:19–31

CALL TO WORSHIP

Come, children of God, to sing a new song;
clap your hands and shout your praise.
**Jesus is our good news,
our joy, and our salvation.**
In steadfast love and faithfulness
God has done marvelous things.
**God raised Jesus from the dead;
Christ is alive and at work among us.**
God calls us into partnership with Christ Jesus
and bids us walk in the light.
**How good and pleasant it is
when brothers and sisters dwell in unity.**

INVOCATION

Breathe your Holy Spirit into this gathering that we may know light and peace. Link us with all your children so we may recognize and celebrate our common humanity rather than quarrel over our differences. Motivate us to share with one another the resources you have entrusted to us. In Jesus' name. Amen.

CALL TO CONFESSION

If we say we have no sin, we deceive ourselves, and the truth of God's word is not in us. We come to confess our sin, knowing that God is faithful and just to forgive us and cleanse us from all unrighteousness.

PRAYER OF CONFESSION

God of Light, you have called us into partnership, but we have chosen instead to go our own way. You have given us light and we have preferred to walk in the shadows. You call us to truth while we cling to our lies. We try to fool others and end up deceiving ourselves. Come to us in our confusion and sin to forgive us, we pray, and make us whole. In Jesus' name. Amen.

ASSURANCE OF FORGIVENESS

Jesus is our advocate with God, the expiation for our sins and those of the whole world. In Christ, God welcomes us to eternal life in which we are partners with God. All who have been cleansed by the blood of Christ are invited to walk in the light as God is light. Amen.

COLLECT

May your word, written that we might believe, lead us to faith in Jesus as God's own child, and bring us to life in Christ's name. Unite us as people of light who minister to one another out of our common need for your truth. Amen.

OFFERTORY INVITATION

We are not really owners of our temporary possessions. Life is a trust from God, who makes us partners in ministry to all creation. Everyone in need has a claim on what we are managing for God. Let us give gladly, grateful for the privilege of sharing.

OFFERTORY PRAYER

Generous God, we respond to your will, that there be no needy among us, by bringing these gifts. May others be brought to faith and wholeness through their use. Unite us all, we pray, in the way of peace. Amen.

COMMISSION AND BLESSING

Walk in light as God's own children,
united in love for one another.
We would dwell in God's house
and abide in Christ's love.
Be guided by God's word,
that you may bear good fruit.
We pray for God's guidance,
that we may love in word and deed.
Peace be with you, as Christ sends you
into the world as God's messengers.
We have received the Holy Spirit
and carry God's message of forgiveness.
Amen.   **Amen.**

(See hymn No. 44.)

Third Sunday of Easter

Historic Message: Acts 3:12–19
                           Psalm 4
Epistle: 1 John 3:1–7
Gospel: Luke 24:35–48

CALL TO WORSHIP

Come, children of God, to sing a new song;
clap your hands and shout for joy.

Jesus is our good news,
our joy, and our salvation.
In steadfast love and faithfulness
God has done marvelous things.
God raised Jesus from the dead;
Christ is alive and at work among us.
God hears our prayers
and answers when we call.
God makes us dwell in safety
and puts joy in our hearts.

INVOCATION

Lift up the light of your countenance on us, O God, for we need the larger view you provide. As we commune with our own hearts we pray that you will heal our distress. Purify our thoughts and actions as we put our trust in you. Through Jesus Christ. Amen.

CALL TO CONFESSION

Sometimes we have acted in ignorance. Often we have been willful children intent on our own lawless way. All of us need to repent and experience forgiveness. Let us come to the Author of Life for the renewal God alone offers us.

PRAYER OF CONFESSION

God of Our Ancestors, God of Today, we come to you in the name of Jesus who lived among us, confessing that we have not been faithful to your purposes. We abide in sin, disdaining the ways of the One who came to take our sin away. We confess that we do not really know Christ or aspire to follow the path of loving service. Heal our brokenness, O God, and bring together the fragments of our scattered existence into a meaningful whole. Amen.

ASSURANCE OF FORGIVENESS

As we repent and turn away from evil, our sins are blotted out. Times of refreshment come from the presence of the Sovereign God, who has heard our cries. God claims us as children of the Most High and offers us a safe haven. Our faith makes us strong to lead others to God's healing power. Amen.

COLLECT

Use our troubled, questioning spirits, O God, to open our understanding of the scriptures. Help us to see the possibilities you set before us as your children when we turn from our lies and live by your truth. Strengthen our faith and our love. Amen.

OFFERTORY INVITATION

We are witnesses to the redeeming activity of Christ in our midst. Our offerings proclaim that depth of our commitment and extend our witness beyond this community to the ends of the earth. Let us give as we have been blessed.

OFFERTORY PRAYER

We give thanks, Gracious God, for the joy of giving our gifts and ourselves. May others find refreshment and wholeness through our sharing. In Jesus' name. Amen.

COMMISSION AND BLESSING

Walk in the light as God's own children,
united in love for one another.
We would dwell in God's house
and abide in Christ's love.
Be guided by God's word,
that you may bear good fruit.
We pray for God's guidance,
that we may love in word and deed.
See what love God has given us;
dare to walk in that love.
O that we might see some good
and show God's goodness to others.
Amen.   **Amen.**

(See hymn No. 45.)

Fourth Sunday of Easter

Historic Message: Acts 4:8–12
                   Psalm 23
Epistle: 1 John 3:18–24
Gospel: John 10:11–18

CALL TO WORSHIP

Come, children of God, to sing a new song;
clap your hands and shout for joy.
Jesus is our good news,
our joy, and our salvation.
In steadfast love and faithfulness
God has done marvelous things.
God raised Jesus from the dead;
Christ is alive and at work among us.
The Rejected One has become faith's cornerstone;
there is salvation in no one else.
No other name is given among earth's people
than Jesus, by whom we are being saved.

INVOCATION

Gentle Shepherd, who knows our hearts' desire and our spirits' need, assure us now of your presence with us, we pray. Claim this time and place as your own that we may not mistakenly view this church as our own possession. Grant us a universal vision that recognizes all your children as members of one family. In Jesus' name. Amen.

CALL TO CONFESSION

Come in confidence that we will receive from God what we ask. The goodness and mercy of God are ours to claim. Let us bring our need for forgiveness and healing to this time of confession.

PRAYER OF CONFESSION

O God, we have listened to voices other than yours and followed in paths of our own making. We have evaded your commandments to do what pleases us. Our hearts condemn us, but we lack the will and the strength to change our ways. Have mercy on us and forgive us, we pray, that we may devote ourselves to doing what pleases you, Our God. We pray in the name of Jesus Christ. Amen.

ASSURANCE OF FORGIVENESS

If we keep the commandments, we abide in God's love and God grants us the Holy Spirit as our guide and comforter. Surely God's goodness and mercy shall follow us all the days of our lives, and we will dwell in God's house forever. Amen.

COLLECT

Loving God, who reaches out to restore our souls, touch us now with your word of truth. May the familiar phrases of scripture draw us back into a vital relationship with you and all your children. Lead us in paths of righteousness that we may show your love in conversation and action. Amen.

OFFERTORY INVITATION

Let us do what pleases God: think beyond ourselves and give to causes greater than our own interests. By God's grace we are never in want. Our abundance is intended for ministry to others' needs. Give, then, in thanksgiving to God and concern for our neighbors.

OFFERTORY PRAYER

You fill our cups to overflowing and empower us for good deeds. Be pleased, O God, to use these tokens of our love for the sake of your whole flock. May our gifts serve to bring others into your fold and equip us all to live fully as your own. Amen.

COMMISSION AND BLESSING

Walk in the light as God's own children,
united in love for one another.

We would dwell in God's house
and abide in Christ's love.
Be guided by God's word,
that you may bear good fruit.
We pray for God's guidance,
that we may love in word and deed.
Be filled with the Holy Spirit
for your own and the world's healing.
We reach out in Christ's name,
inviting others to know the Great Shepherd.
Amen.   Amen.

(See hymn No. 46.)

Fifth Sunday of Easter

Historic Message: Acts 8:26–40
                    Psalm 22:25–31
Epistle: 1 John 4:7–12
Gospel: John 15:1–8

CALL TO WORSHIP

Come, children of God, to sing a new song,
clap your hands and shout for joy.
Jesus is our good news,
our joy, and our salvation.
In steadfast love and faithfulness
God has done marvelous things.
God raised Jesus from the dead;
Christ is alive and at work among us.
The ends of the earth turn to God;
all families of nations worship our Creator.
Christ is the vine; we are the branches.
Apart from Christ we can do nothing.

INVOCATION

We come to you, Loving God, needing the love you alone can give. Your
love comes to us in Jesus, bringing abundant life for all who will receive
it. Empower us by your love to love one another; abide in us to perfect
your gift within and among us. Through Christ. Amen.

CALL TO CONFESSION

Come, all the proud of the earth, to bow down before our Creator. Come, all who think we can live for ourselves, to reestablish our relationship with God. Come, all who are alienated from sisters and brothers, to rejoin the human family. Let us pray.

PRAYER OF CONFESSION

We confess, O God, that we are accustomed to having our own way. Our abundance has tricked us into believing that we are independent, self-sustaining creatures. Yet, when our ingenuity solves one problem, a dozen more seem to take its place. We need help to understand, to be reconnected, to be truly productive. We need your love and forgiveness in order to live with ourselves, and with one another. Help us, God! Amen.

ASSURANCE OF FORGIVENESS

God takes away branches that bear no fruit and prunes others that they may flourish. We are grafted into the true vine for the nourishment we need. Abide in Christ and receive the spoken word that cleanses and empowers. Ask anything, as Christ's disciples, and it will be done, for God's love is being perfected in us. Amen.

COLLECT

Interpret your word to us, Gracious God, so we can understand and act. Feed us with food that satisfies and cleanse us from all that pollutes and destroys. May we be productive branches of the true vine, Jesus Christ, subject to your love and care. Confront and shape us according to your perfect love. Amen.

OFFERTORY INVITATION

Beloved, let us love one another because God has first loved us and given Jesus as the expiation for our sin. In joyous gratitude we accept the privilege of making a generous response. May God bless and multiply our gifts, and increase in us the joy of sharing.

OFFERTORY PRAYER

We give to tell the world your good news in Christ. As you have loved us, we give ourselves in love for all your people. May we glorify you through our discipleship. Amen.

COMMISSION AND BLESSING

Walk in the light as God's own children,
united in love for one another.
**We would dwell in God's house
and abide in Christ's love.**
Be guided by God's word,
that you may bear good fruit.
**We pray for God's guidance,
that we may love in word and deed.**

The Spirit of Christ
sends you on your way rejoicing.
All the ends of the earth are responding
to what God has done for us in Christ.
Amen.   **Amen.**

(See hymn No. 47.)

Sixth Sunday of Easter

Historic Message: Acts 10:44–48
Psalm 98
Epistle: 1 John 5:1–6
Gospel: John 15:9–17

CALL TO WORSHIP

Sing a new song to God,
who has done marvelous things.
We celebrate God's steadfast love
and rejoice in God's faithfulness.
Make a joyful noise to God, all the earth;
break forth in songs of praise.
With lyre and trumpets and horns,
we make melody in thanks to God.
Rejoice that God has come in Jesus Christ
to call us beloved friends.
We sing for joy that Christ chooses us
to go out and bear much fruit.

INVOCATION

Amazing God, whose voice we hear in unexpected places, among persons who seem unlikely witnesses, we come together to renew our commitment and sing your praise. We rejoice in your love poured out in Jesus Christ, whereby we are equipped to overcome the world. Grant us your Spirit in this hour, we pray. Amen.

CALL TO CONFESSION

God comes to judge the earth with righteousness and the people with equity. We can bring our failures and wrongdoing to God, knowing that God will receive us fairly and help us to overcome our sin.

PRAYER OF CONFESSION

O God, we have not lived as your servants; how can we ever aspire to be

Jesus' friends? We complain rather than sing your praises. We ignore your commandments and dismiss them as unimportant. We focus on our own self-interest rather than giving ourselves for causes and people important to your purposes. Turn us around, God, and help us to devote ourselves to your way. In Jesus' name. Amen.

ASSURANCE OF FORGIVENESS

Whatever you ask of God may be given you. The Holy Spirit comes among us, bringing assurance of God's forgiveness and changing past distinctions. Abide in God's love. You have been chosen to be Christ's friend and appointed to bear much fruit. Amen.

COLLECT

We come to your word with faith and expectation, seeking to know what you want us to learn and do. Teach us your commandments and surround us with your love that we may know the joy of serving you. Grant us your transforming Spirit, we pray. Amen.

OFFERTORY INVITATION

The marvelous works of God that surround us and give meaning to life call for our generous response. How shall we return God's love? Surely, in part, by loving others through the programs and outreach of the church. Let us give as God has given to us.

OFFERTORY PRAYER

Thank you, God, for the joy of loving and giving, for the friendship of Christ and the opportunities you give us to serve. May these gifts be used in accordance with your love for all your people. In Jesus' name. Amen.

COMMISSION AND BLESSING

Walk in the light as God's own children,
united in love for one another.
We would dwell in God's house
and abide in Christ's love.
Be guided by God's word,
that you may bear good fruit.
We pray for God's guidance,
that we may love in word and deed.
Receive God's new birth to strengthen your faith,
the Holy Spirit to empower your witness.
We go forth as friends of Christ,
empowered by God's love to love others.
Amen.   **Amen.**

(See hymn No. 48.)

Ascension
(or Seventh Sunday of Easter)

Historic Message: Acts 1:1–11
Psalm 47
Epistle: Ephesians 1:15–23
Gospel: Luke 24:46–53

CALL TO WORSHIP

Clap your hands, all peoples,
shout to God with loud songs of joy.
Sing praise to God, sing praises,
for Christ is alive and the Holy Spirit comes.
God is ruler over all the earth
and reigns over all nations.
God put all things under Christ's feet;
Christ is head over all things for the church.
Gather to know the immeasurable greatness of God,
to exalt in the One who grants revelation.
We come together blessing God
for all we have seen and heard.

INVOCATION

We enter into worship with great joy, O God, for you grant us acceptance
and lift us up with visions of what is yet to be. Hear our psalms of praise
and songs of faith as we wait in anticipation for the power of your Spirit
among us and within. Bless our worship. In Jesus' name. Amen.

CALL TO CONFESSION

We who are called to preach repentance and forgiveness to all nations,
take time to recognize sin in ourselves. We need to confess our sin, to find
pardon and peace. Let us join together in private and public confession.

PRAYER OF CONFESSION

Ruler of Heaven and Earth, we confess that we would like to regulate
your timetables and shape your plans. We prefer our ways to the unknown design of your realm and purposes. We aspire to recognition more
than faithfulness, and to an insider's role more than an inclusive community for all your children. Forgive our pretensions and restore us to
right relationships with you and all your people. In Jesus' name. Amen.

ASSURANCE OF FORGIVENESS

God rules over all the earth and reigns over all the nations. Those who do
not believe are condemned, but to all who believe there is offered the

immeasurable greatness of God's power. Receive God's forgiveness with joy! Amen.

COLLECT

O God, whose times and seasons are beyond our knowing, open the eyes of our hearts to today's revelation, that we may be enlightened by wisdom and hope. We who are slow to believe rejoice that we are called to be the Body of Christ, going into all the world to share the gospel. Bless us by your promises and by the power of the Holy Spirit. Amen.

OFFERTORY INVITATION

God, who is ruler over all the earth, bids us manage well the time and substance placed in our hands. We are called to be stewards of all we possess, and to return for Christ's Body, the church, a portion, to extend discipleship everywhere. Let us give with joy!

OFFERTORY PRAYER

We respond as your apostles to the mission on which you send us. As we speak of your realm, we would also extend the outreach of others on behalf of your whole church in every land. We give thanks for your revelation and your rule. Inspire your church to use these gifts to your glory. Amen.

COMMISSION AND BLESSING

Carry God's promises to all you meet
and proclaim God's immeasurable greatness.
The eyes of our hearts have been enlightened,
and we know the hope to which we are called.
Christ blesses you with uplifted hands,
granting insight and wisdom.
We sing praises to God in word and deed,
for Christ is alive and the Spirit comes.
You shall receive power from the Holy Spirit
to be witnesses to the ends of the earth.
May our speech and our work be confirmed by God,
that the world may hear and believe.
Amen. **Amen.**

(See hymn No. 49.)

Seventh Sunday of Easter

Historic Message: Acts 1:15–17, 21–26
Psalm 1
Epistle: 1 John 5:9–13
Gospel: John 17:11b–19

CALL TO WORSHIP

Come, children of God, to sing a new song;
clap your hands and shout for joy.
Jesus is our good news,
our joy, and our salvation.
In steadfast love and faithfulness
God has done marvelous things.
God raised Jesus from the dead;
Christ is alive and at work among us.
Blessed are those who seek good counsel
and avoid scoffing and sin's fragmentation.
We will delight in the law of God
and meditate on it day and night.

INVOCATION

Eternal God, who gathers a congregation of the righteous, grant us to stand among your people. We are here to listen to your testimony and share in the life of faith. We believe; help our unbelief, and prepare us to be disciples of Jesus, in whose name we pray. Amen.

CALL TO CONFESSION

We stand before God, whose judgment is sure, not wanting to think of ourselves as wicked or lost. Let us pray that we may be kept from evil and sanctified in the truth.

PRAYER OF CONFESSION

Sovereign God, save us from the fate of Judas, who wanted to control events in his own way. Rescue us from the scoffers' seat and the way of sinners. Guard and protect us from doubts and lies. We confess our involvement in all these conditions, and our reluctance to change. Liberate us from our confusion and brokenness, for we cannot truly live as we are. Change us, God, before we are so hardened we cannot change. We pray in Jesus' name. Amen.

ASSURANCE OF FORGIVENESS

God gives us eternal life in Jesus Christ, beginning here and now for all who repent and believe. Christ prays that we be kept from evil. Let us turn away, then, from the chaff of injustice to the righteousness of our Creator. Accept God's sovereignty and delight in God's law. Amen.

COLLECT
Guide us, O God, to find those leaders who will direct us in the way of discipleship. Make us like trees, planted by streams of living water, absorbing your testimony and living by your truth. Grant us now your word that we may be sanctified and kept in your name. Amen.

OFFERTORY INVITATION
Come with your offerings to spread the joy of God's word and bear testimony to God's gift of eternal life. Let us prepare to consecrate ourselves with our gifts.

OFFERTORY PRAYER
Send us and our offerings where they are needed in your world, O God. May we witness to Christ's resurrection, be apostles of your love, and share eternal life with one another. Expand our joy in giving ourselves, our substance, and the truth of your word. Amen.

COMMISSION AND BLESSING
Walk in light as God's own children,
united in love for one another.
We would dwell in God's house
and abide in Christ's love.
Be guided by God's word,
that you may bear good fruit.
We pray for God's guidance,
that we may love in word and deed.
Delight in God's law and share God's love
as disciples of the risen Christ.
The testimony of God's truth dwells in us
and compels our speaking and serving.
Amen.   **Amen.**

(See hymn No. 50.)

The Pentecost Season

Pentecost Sunday

Old Testament: Ezekiel 37:1–14
Psalm 104:24–34
Epistle: Acts 2:1–21
Gospel: John 15:26–27; 16:4b–15

CALL TO WORSHIP

O God, how manifold are your works!
In wisdom you have made them all;
the earth is full of your creatures.
These look to you,
to give them their food in due season.
When you open your hand,
they are filled with good things.
When you send forth your Spirit, they are created;
and you renew the face of the ground.
Let us sing to God as long as we live,
sing praises to our God while we have being.
May our meditation be pleasing to God,
in whom we rejoice.

INVOCATION

Sweep through our midst, Mighty Wind, to give us new breath. Awaken
our spirits, inspire our praise, set us on fire with your love. May no one
here remain unmoved by your presence or cut off from the dreams you
inspire. Amen.

CALL TO CONFESSION

Come, all who are content, and all who live in hopeless despair. Come
before the Creator and Life-giver, who knows you as you are and is
waiting to respond to your pleas. Let us confess our sin.

PRAYER OF CONFESSION

Merciful God, we have cut ourselves off from the power of your presence,
lest we be swept off our feet and be forced to see life from a new
perspective. We have belittled those who speak with certainty of your
transforming Spirit and turned away from any truth larger than our own
perceptions. We are dry bones in a valley of dry bones. How shall we
live? Amen.

ASSURANCE OF FORGIVENESS

God's Spirit comes, and we are filled with the breath of life. Our sons and daughters prophesy. The young see visions and the old dream dreams. Whoever calls on God will be saved. Accept the truth of God in your inner being, and rejoice that God fills you with all good things. Amen.

COLLECT

O God, you have spoken, and we have received the gift of life. You have opened your hand and we have been fed. You have touched us with fire and our tongues have been loosened to sing your praise. You have opened the ears of your people and barriers to understanding have come tumbling down. Guide us now in your truth that we may hear all you wish to declare to us. In Jesus' name. Amen.

OFFERTORY INVITATION

God, who has given us food in due season, calls us to share our bread with the hungry. In the name of the One who lived God's truth among us, we commit ourselves anew to bearing witness. The Holy Spirit, whose winds restore our breath, sends us forth as life-givers. Celebrate this opportunity to give!

OFFERTORY PRAYER

Thank you, God, for this high moment in worship and in life when we have something to give that others need. Take our bread, our witness, our lives to benefit all your human family. May your glory be known among us and in all the world. Amen.

COMMISSION AND BLESSING

Embark on another week of service,
filled with the hope that the Spirit brings.
**We who have the first fruits of the Spirit
groan inwardly as we await our adoption.**
God redeems and accepts us
and sends the Spirit to help us in our weakness.
**We sense the Spirit helping us to pray,
interceding for us with sighs too deep for words.**
The One who searches human hearts
knows the mind of the Spirit.
**We are saints of God, whom the Spirit claims,
children of the Most High in whom we rejoice.**
Amen.   **Amen.**

(See hymn No. 51.)

Trinity Sunday

CALL TO WORSHIP

God comes in the wind and thunder and flame,
changing the circumstances of our lives.
Holy, holy, holy is the God of hosts;
the whole earth is full of God's glory.
God reveals to us the things of heaven and earth,
pointing us to the realm of God.
We speak of what we know,
and bear witness to what we have seen.
God so loved the world that God gave
Jesus Christ to live among us and die for us.
When we cry out to God, the Spirit bears witness
that we are children of God and heirs with Christ.

INVOCATION

Lead us by your Spirit that we may become, in all ways, your sons and
daughters. We stand in awe before your majesty and bow in fear before
your power. Yet we are also assured by your promises and lifted up by
your strength. Meet us now in the midst of our earthly concerns to point
us toward the eternal. Amen.

CALL TO CONFESSION

The foundations shake at God's voice, and the wilderness trembles before
God's power. In awe and expectation we come before the only One who
can make sense of our lives and restore us to wholeness.

PRAYER OF CONFESSION

"Woe is me! For I am lost; for I am a person of unclean lips, and I dwell in
the midst of a people of unclean lips." Holy God, we have lived as people
enslaved to the gods of this world, victims of our own misplaced passions.
We have embraced the ways of death and turned from the challenge of
rebirth. The paths we have chosen lead to dead ends, and the direction
we have followed brings only confusion and despair. Help us, O God, for
we cannot help ourselves. Amen.

ASSURANCE OF FORGIVENESS

With a burning coal, God touches our lips and burns away the guilt within us. God's forgiveness puts to death our self-preoccupation and frees us for new life. Whoever believes may have eternal life, for God sent Jesus into the world, not to condemn the world, but to secure our salvation. Our guilt is taken away, and our sin is forgiven. Rejoice in the gift! Amen.

COLLECT

From your throne, high and lifted up, your voice, O God, thunders among us, calling us out of slavery and death to freedom and new life. May we who are born of the flesh be born anew by the Spirit. Grant us to experience the Wind that blows where it will, that we may hear all you want us to hear. Amen.

OFFERTORY INVITATION

We who can come to Jesus in the light of day rather than in the hiddenness of night, give thanks and give ourselves in this act of sharing. As debtors to God we are invited to return a portion of God's bounty to proclaim the good news of peace. Let us bring our tithes and offerings.

OFFERTORY PRAYER

We join you, Holy God, in offering strength to all your people. We would devote our resources to realization of family in the midst of our human diversity, for you have been as a parent to us all. Now, as we share our financial resources, we pray that you will engage us in a pattern of sharing that will give new significance and meaning to our days. Amen.

COMMISSION AND BLESSING

Be led forth by the Spirit
as sons and daughters of the Living God.
We are enslaved to no one or no thing,
for we are heirs with Christ of God's bounty.
We are a people born of water and of the Spirit,
who are sent out as witnesses to the world.
May God give strength to us and to all people;
may God bless the world with peace.
Receive the promises of God,
and know eternal life in the midst of time.
We hear God calling us to lives of service,
and we reply, "Here am I! Send me."
Amen.   **Amen.**

(See hymn No. 52.)

Pentecost 2
(May 29—June 4, if After Trinity)

Old Testament: 1 Samuel 16:1–13
Psalm 20
Epistle: 2 Corinthians 4:5–12
Gospel: Mark 2:23—3:6

CALL TO WORSHIP

Bring to God your sacrifices of praise
and the consecration of your hearts.
Help comes from God's sanctuary;
God answers us in our day of trouble.
God causes us to rise and stand upright
and fills our lives with new purpose.
Light shines in our darkness,
and we know God's glory in the face of Christ.
Look beyond these earthen vessels that we are
to know the transcendent power of God.
May the Spirit come mightily among us
to heal and grant new life.

INVOCATION

O God, before whom there are no secrets, we approach you as we really
are, in all our brokenness and hardness of heart, in all our pretense and
pride. Come into the darkness we have created with the light of your
glory, that we may worship you with our whole being. Through Jesus
Christ. Amen.

CALL TO CONFESSION

Come, people of God, to confess all that separates you from God and from
other people—whether proud boasts or anguished despair, hidden deceits or arrogant pretensions. We cannot truly worship until we have faced
ourselves before God and admitted our need for help.

PRAYER OF CONFESSION

Help us, O God, to see ourselves as you see us. We admit before you our
prejudices, our harsh judgment of others, and the excuses we make for
our own sin. We prefer our own arrangements to your designs for human
fulfillment. We harden our hearts against those who most need a helping
hand and understanding presence. O God, enlarge our capacity for truth
and compassion. Save us from our worst selves to realize the best you
intend for us. In Jesus' name. Amen.

ASSURANCE OF FORGIVENESS

As Jesus reached out in healing love to those who sought relief from their suffering, God comes now to all who earnestly seek a new life. Our Creator fills these earthen vessels with God's own glory. The Spirit lifts us up and restores us to wholeness. Praise God! Amen.

COLLECT

Let the light of your word shine into the darkness of our world, illuminating our choices, enlightening our actions, and empowering our service. Melt the hardness of our hearts, expanding our compassion and enlarging the circle of our concern. We listen for your voice of peace and await knowledge of your glory in the face of Christ. Amen.

OFFERTORY INVITATION

Our worth is not in our belongings, but in our benevolences. In passing on God's providence, more than in possessing the products of our labor, we find our true identity. Let us give, therefore, because this act benefits us as well as those we would help. Let us give because the God who has blessed us is honored through our offerings.

OFFERTORY PRAYER

Make our sacrifices of thanksgiving and grateful response into instruments of your purposes, O God, for we would be consecrated, along with our gifts. Remember all our offerings with your favor, that they may serve your purposes for humanity. In Jesus' name. Amen.

COMMISSION AND BLESSING

Go forth, looking at all you meet with new eyes,
filled with compassion for all who suffer.
We would see with the eyes of Christ
and reach out to others with helping hands.
Use the earthen vessels of your lives
to show the transcendent power of God.
We carry within us the death of Jesus,
that the life of Jesus may be manifested in us.
God has made this day for your growth
and goes with you every day to give life.
The Spirit of God has come to us,
granting fulfillment of our highest desires.
Amen.   **Amen.**

(See hymn No. 53.)

Pentecost 3
(June 5–11, if After Trinity)

Old Testament: 1 Samuel 16:14–23
Psalm 57
Epistle: 2 Corinthians 4:13—5:1
Gospel: Mark 3:20–35

CALL TO WORSHIP

Assemble with songs on your lips
and expectation in your hearts.
Be exalted, O God, above the heavens,
and let your glory be over all the earth.
Look not to things that are seen,
but to realities that are unseen.
For things that are seen are transient,
but things that are unseen are eternal.
Give thanks to God among all the people;
praise God among all nations.
God's steadfast love and faithfulness
lift us up and save us.

INVOCATION

Spirit of the Living God, be with us here, lest we depart from your
purposes and lose heart in the face of affliction. Soothe our hurts and
renew our inner nature so we may serve as sisters and brothers of Jesus
Christ, in whose name we pray. Amen.

CALL TO CONFESSION

The more we walk with Christ, the more we realize our desperate need
for forgiveness and healing. Sometimes we seem in the grip of forces
beyond our control, while at other times we knowingly pursue what is
evil and destructive. God does not turn away from us when we fail, but
eagerly awaits our return. Come to God with all your burden of wrongdoing and acknowledgment of good left undone.

PRAYER OF CONFESSION

Be merciful to us, O God, for we have wandered from your ways and
pursued the gods of this world. We are more concerned with position and
success than with service and faithfulness. We are frightened by the
storms of life and begin to lose heart, as if we had no one but ourselves on
whom to rely. We blame you for the destruction we bring on ourselves
and challenge your design for living without trying it. We are torn apart

by our own inconsistencies and contradictions. Have mercy on us, O God, and help us. Amen.

ASSURANCE OF FORGIVENESS

All our sin is forgiven as we turn away from it with new resolve. In grace and mercy God raises us up with Jesus to realities not made with hands, eternal in the heavens. Our salvation is assured. We are healed and refreshed. Join in the music that transcends all our lesser tunes! Amen.

COLLECT

Great God of rulers and commoners, good and evil, young and old, rich and poor, we come to your word. It challenges our previous assumptions and calls for our undivided attention. May we find in these lessons your purposes for us and the love that moves us toward realization of your will. We believe. Shape and inform our speech and our actions. Through Jesus Christ. Amen.

OFFERTORY INVITATION

Each of us has talents to share and resources to invest in God's service. In thankfulness may we bring our gifts and ourselves as our offering to God.

OFFERTORY PRAYER

As people in other cultures have brought gifts to their rulers, we bring our outpouring of thanksgiving and the products of our labor to you, O God. May our offerings and our service bring glory to your name. Amen.

COMMISSION AND BLESSING

Embark on another week as God's own,
in the grace God gives in Christ.
Because we believe, we go out to speak,
knowing that God will raise us with Jesus.
God sends us forth in steadfast love,
standing by us in faithfulness and support.
We will not lose heart in the face of affliction,
or give in to discouragement when opposed.
Whoever does the will of God
is part of the family of Jesus Christ.
With steadfast hearts and eager anticipation
we enter the joys and challenges of this week.
Amen.   **Amen.**

(See hymn No. 54.)

Pentecost 4
(June 12–18, if After Trinity)

Old Testament: 2 Samuel 1:1, 17–27
Psalm 46
Epistle: 2 Corinthians 5:6–10, 14–17
Gospel: Mark 4:26–34

CALL TO WORSHIP
Come, all who are troubled or weary,
who know the pain of the world's people.
God is our refuge and strength,
a very present help in trouble.
As we gather we affirm God's presence
and seek to know as we are known.
The God of hosts is with us;
the God of our ancestors hears and leads us.
Be still and know that God is God,
exalted among the nations of this earth.
The realm of God is here and everywhere,
in time and beyond time.

INVOCATION
Quiet our busy minds and fearful hearts, O God, that we may be still before your awesome majesty. Speak to us in our grief, when the foundations of our existence are shaken and we cannot see beyond the present moment. Grant us courage to go forward by faith, not by sight. In Jesus' name. Amen.

CALL TO CONFESSION
The apostle Paul tells us we must all appear before the judgment seat of Christ to receive good or evil, according to what we have done in the body. But there are more immediate results from our confession. God's way of integrity and faithfulness is the only way that works. That way alone provides fulfillment and abundant life. We come to God needing to be freed from the oppression of our wrongdoing and from haunting guilt over the good we have left undone. Let us pour out our sin before God.

PRAYER OF CONFESSION
We confess before you, O God, our misplaced anger, which originates from viewing people and events as satellites of ourselves. We like to have our own way, God, and are upset when others don't fit into our plans. We are content with our privileges and are seldom disturbed by inequalities

that are tipped to our own advantage. Forgive us, O God, for living for ourselves and regarding others from a human point of view. Tune us in to the mind of Christ. Amen.

ASSURANCE OF FORGIVENESS

Anyone who is in Christ is a new creation. The old has passed away; the new has come. Christ died for all, that those who live in Christ may no longer live only for themselves. Let us respond as forgiven sinners, set free from our bondage to self, to live and act within the love of Christ. Amen.

COLLECT

Amid the troubles and threats of a world trembling on the brink of destructive forces, we look to your word, O God, for assurance and guidance. Our eyes see desolation on every hand, but we would set our feet on the way of faith and hope. Sow within us and others the seeds of a new day when your realm is acknowledged and realized in our midst. Amen.

OFFERTORY INVITATION

What will we give to witness to Christ's presence amid the world's pain? How much of our wealth will we share to proclaim the realm of God among the nations of this world? Where will the good news of a caring God reach because of our giving? We hold the answers in our hands.

OFFERTORY PRAYER

God of Hosts, receive our gifts and create new miracles in our church and our world. Unite us in a faith that sees beyond the mustard seed contributions of today to the mighty plant that gives support, protection, and peace. Bring your realm among us and within each one, we pray. Amen.

COMMISSION AND BLESSING

Live as God's people in the world:
forgiven, supported, loved, equipped to serve.
God is our refuge and strength,
a very present help in trouble.
Affirm God's presence in desperate places,
and open the eyes of others to God's love.
The God of hosts is with us;
the God of our ancestors hears and leads us.
Be still and know that God is God.
Claim God's realm for one another.
The realm of God is everywhere,
in time and beyond time.
Amen.   **Amen.**

(See hymns No. 55 and No. 56.)

Pentecost 5
(June 19–25, if After Trinity)

Old Testament: 2 Samuel 5:1–5
Psalm 48
Epistle: 2 Corinthians 5:18—6:2
Gospel: Mark 4:35–41

CALL TO WORSHIP

Behold, now is the acceptable time;
behold, now is the day of salvation.
Great is God and greatly to be praised;
all the ends of the earth know God's name.
We have heard and seen God's steadfast love
in the sacrifice of Jesus Christ for us.
Through Christ we are reconciled to God,
who does not count our trespasses against us.
Come, then, rejoicing and praising God
in awe and wonder and faith.
The storms of life cannot destroy
our Savior's "Peace, be still."

6/19/88

✓ INVOCATION   *Prayer before Worship*

O God, Our thoughts and emotions are lifted up, Gracious God, to the heights of
your holy mountain from which we behold a beauty our eyes cannot see.
You are our sure defense before all life's perils and our resting place when
the storms of life are past. We are drawn to worship by a presence beyond
our knowing and a love too majestic for words to describe. Draw us now
to the source of our being that we may be renewed in every way. Amen.

CALL TO CONFESSION

Behold, now is the acceptable time; behold, now is the day of salvation.
This is the moment when we need to be cleansed from all our past sin and
empowered to meet God's new day in freedom and joy. Come to receive
the fresh start God offers us.

PRAYER OF CONFESSION

How great you are, O God! Before your majesty we are astonished. We
tremble when we consider the ways we have failed you, and panic when
we take account of the judgment you might pronounce against us. Hear
us as, in silence, we confess the sin that separates us from you and from
one another. . . . Heal us and make us whole, that Christ's sacrifice may
not be in vain. Amen.

ASSURANCE OF FORGIVENESS

Through Christ we are reconciled to God, who does not count our trespasses against us. For our sake God made Christ to be sin, who knew no sin, that in Christ we might become the righteousness of God. We who are reconciled are now called to be God's messengers of reconciliation. Amen.

COLLECT

Great Shepherd of rulers and commoners, saints and sinners, disciples and detractors, lead us now to hear and see and think about your steadfast love. As we accept your grace may we work with you to reconcile persons to one another. May each of us claim your gift of reconciliation and live in community, even with those with whom we disagree. Confront us now with the One whom even wind and sea obey. Amen.

OFFERTORY INVITATION

Because God surrounds us with steadfast love, because we are people of faith, because we care about others who are perishing, we bring offerings to support the work of our church. Let us join together to publish the message of reconciliation wherever our influence can reach.

OFFERTORY PRAYER

Thank you, Great Shepherd, for your grace and guidance in bringing us close to God and to our sisters and brothers. You have helped us to recognize the good in ourselves and in other people. We have come to appreciate this present moment as a unique and valuable gift. Now we dedicate all our moments and all our days to your service as part of our offering. Bless each gift and giver, we pray. Amen.

✓ COMMISSION AND BLESSING   6/19/88

On this day of our salvation
we go forth to praise God everywhere.
We have heard and seen God's steadfast love
in the sacrifice of Jesus Christ for us.
Christ goes with us as guide and protector,
calming the winds and granting us peace.
In stillness or in storm we will not panic,
For Jesus Christ calms our fears.
God entrusts to us the message of reconciliation,
appealing to the world through us.
We are ambassadors for Christ,
in whom God's grace is shared with humanity.
Amen.   **Amen.**

(See hymn No. 57.)

Pentecost 6
(June 26–July 2)

Old Testament: 2 Samuel 6:1–15
Psalm 24
Epistle: 2 Corinthians 8:7–15
Gospel: Mark 5:21–43

CALL TO WORSHIP

Lift up your heads, O people of God,
to meet the Glorious Ruler of all worlds.
The earth is God's and the fullness thereof,
the world and all who dwell therein.
Who shall ascend to the hill of God,
and who shall stand in God's holy place?
Those who have clean hands and pure hearts,
who are not false or deceitful.
Make merry before God with all your being;
praise God with instruments and singing.
We celebrate the abundance of God's blessings
and respond to God with all we have to give.

INVOCATION

O God of Hosts, draw near to us in our need and bless us with your presence. Quiet our fears before your Holy Majesty and surround us with your grace. So lift us up in this time of worship that we may serve confidently as representatives of your realm. In Jesus' name. Amen.

CALL TO CONFESSION

We who have mishandled the sacred gift of life, while conspiring to control the course of events in our own favor, are called to this time of confession. The more we know of God, the more we realize how far short we fall of God's purposes for us. Come to God in honest self-examination and desire to live as God intends.

PRAYER OF CONFESSION

Almighty Ruler, we have tried to hide from you our self-concern, deceits, and dirty hands. Because we do not see great evil within us, we turn away from confession of sin. Our minor flaws seem insignificant before the horrors we discern on every hand. We find it hard to accept responsibility for the inequities that enrich some and impoverish others in a world where you claim all human beings equally as your children. Convict us of our responsibility and our need for your salvation in Christ, in whose name we pray for forgiveness and insight. Amen.

ASSURANCE OF FORGIVENESS

We will receive blessing and vindication from the God of our salvation. When we face the truth about ourselves, God takes us by the hand and proclaims, "Your faith has made you well." Go, therefore, and sin no more. Amen.

COLLECT

Open our eyes, we pray, to the transforming power of your presence. We reach out once more to receive the gift of abundant life. Cleanse our thoughts and actions so our love may be genuine and our dedication to your service, complete. Bless every household here represented with your word of truth. Through Christ. Amen.

OFFERTORY INVITATION

We have received blessings from God; how will we show our gratitude? We are called to give as we are able; how will we respond? We are invited to life that can be embraced only as it is shared; how much are we prepared to give?

OFFERTORY PRAYER

Amazing God, who has entrusted to us the gift of your good earth, enable our stewardship. Set before us once more the example of Christ, who left the riches of your realm to become poor for our sakes. Thank you for that gift and for the assurance that our sharing can supply others' needs without impoverishing us. Move us to genuine love and faithful service. In Jesus' name. Amen.

COMMISSION AND BLESSING

Depart from this place with singing,
for God goes with you in your serving.
All the earth belongs to God;
we cannot escape from God's intent.
Do not be afraid to climb or to reach out,
to ask for what you need, or to dare the new.
God's grace is sufficient for all our desires,
and God's mercy abounds for all our needs.
Rejoice, then, in your work and play,
serving God with genuine love for all.
We will share the riches of Christ
with all whom we meet.
Amen.   **Amen.**

(See hymn No. 58.)

Pentecost 7
(July 3–9)

Old Testament: 2 Samuel 7:1–17
Psalm 89:20–37
Epistle: 2 Corinthians 12:1–10
Gospel: Mark 6:1–6

CALL TO WORSHIP

God is with us wherever we go;
let us together recognize God's presence here.
God is the Creator of our lives
and does not abandon us on life's pilgrimage.
God relates to us as a Parent,
loving, chastening, and disciplining.
We have known the steadfast love of God
when we are faithful and when we stray.
We live in covenant with God,
who is our rock and our salvation.
We hear God calling us to covenant renewal,
offering us strength to overcome our weaknesses.

INVOCATION

Draw us near to you, that we may recognize your all-sustaining love and power, O God. Come to us in our weakness and vulnerability, that we may face with new confidence the hardships and calamities of life. Help us to hear the wisdom resident among us as we listen to one another. May each of us be channels of your revelation and willingly acknowledge your presence and guidance as it comes in unexpected times, places, and people. Amen.

CALL TO CONFESSION

All our schemes are not God's schemes. Our grand designs for our lives may not reflect God's intent for us. The roles we project on others may violate God's purposes for them. So we recognize together our need to reorder our thinking and acting—and to be freed from our past mistakes. Let us seek God's forgiveness.

PRAYER OF CONFESSION

We confess, O God, our repeated tendency to insist on our own way. We want to make a name for ourselves no matter who is hurt by our pursuit of fame. We want you to cater to our needs and our schemes, and we're upset when you do not ease the way for us. Forgive our unwillingness to listen when your word comes to us through parents, children, friends, and humble messengers. Open our ears and help us to discern when you are speaking, and when the popular advice around us is not of your will and purpose. In Jesus' name. Amen.

ASSURANCE OF FORGIVENESS

Let us hear, with the apostle Paul, the assurance of God: "My grace is sufficient for you, for my power is made perfect in weakness." God receives us and accepts us where we are, offering to guide us toward authentic personhood and meaningful service. God continues in covenant with us, inviting our conscious response and faithfulness. Amen.

COLLECT

Be with us, God, as your word unfolds before us in ancient words, made new by personal encounter. May we sense your faithfulness through the generations, surrounding and upholding us. Meet us in our weakness with your strength, in our denials with your affirmation, and in our failures with renewed vision. By your grace we are being reached even now by your salvation. Amen.

OFFERTORY INVITATION

God awaits our response to all we have seen and heard. Our offerings are symbols of our commitment or our unbelief, our willingness to share or our self-preoccupation. Do all that is in your heart; God is with you.

OFFERTORY PRAYER

Move us, O God, beyond the building of monuments to our faith to participation in mission, beyond the giving of our money to the giving of ourselves. Help us to discern your revelation and to share it. Guide us as we seek to follow Christ among those who know us best and in the company of strangers, that our very being may be our finest offering. Amen.

COMMISSION AND BLESSING

You have experienced once more
the steadfast love of God.
    God is with us wherever we go,
    so we will seek to walk with God this week.
God is our Rock and our Salvation,
available whenever we call.
    When we are weak, God gives us strength;
    in hardship and calamity, God sees us through.
Live, then, as people of the covenant,
in touch moment by moment with the Source of Life.
    God will not fail us or forsake us;
    we are free to live as God's own people.
Amen.   **Amen.**

(See hymn No. 59.)

Pentecost 8
(July 10–16)

Old Testament: 2 Samuel 7:18–29
Psalm 132:11–18
Epistle: Ephesians 1:1–10
Gospel: Mark 6:7–13

CALL TO WORSHIP

Who are we, God, that you have brought us this far?
You have blessed our homes and our church.
You provide bread to satisfy our hunger
and keep us day by day in your covenant.
You have spoken to us in words of promise
and placed a lighted lamp on our way.
You have granted us wisdom and insight
into the mystery of your will.
Let us explore together what this means
for our daily lives and for our church.
We seek to know God's presence here
and to receive spiritual blessings.

INVOCATION

In our journey through life we need to know, O God, that we are not
alone. We hear your promise to be with us in all life's ups and downs, and
in that assurance we seek to be your people. You are great, O God; there
is none like you. Direct us away from the false gods we create so we can
be fully open to your leading as we worship together. Amen.

CALL TO CONFESSION

In the midst of our comfortable routines of decent living we are tempted
to a false pride that sees ourselves as holy and blameless. Yet our relationship with God is not all it should be, and our human contacts are less
than perfect. When we sense the wonder of who God is, we are moved to
admit our unworthiness.

PRAYER OF CONFESSION

We confess, O Sovereign God, to the doubts mixed in with our faith. You
have brought us a long way through life, but there have been many hard
times when you seem to have forgotten us. We have doubted your word,
denied your love, and violated the promises we have made to you. Lift us
out of the narrow circles of self-concern that imprison us in limited vision
and flawed wisdom. Confront us with mystery powerful enough to change
us. Amen.

ASSURANCE OF FORGIVENESS

God has adopted us through Christ and pours out grace to heal and save us. We are redeemed and forgiven, according to God's purposes, revealed in Jesus Christ. We are chosen for discipleship and sent out as ambassadors of good news. Let us live the truth! Amen.

COLLECT

Empower us here to accept the authority and mission you entrust to us. Bring out the greatness you have implanted within, so we may truly be your people. Keep us in your covenant and bless us with every spiritual blessing in Christ. Amen.

OFFERTORY INVITATION

What shall we return to God for grace so freely given and love so lavishly bestowed? Let us extend spiritual blessings we have received to the poor in our midst. Let us feed the hungry and find ourselves fed in ways beyond our imagining.

OFFERTORY PRAYER

For the greatness you have wrought among us, for your word of truth tailored to our limited understanding, for our adoption in Christ, we give thanks with these gifts. Grant that our offering may reach those who most need the help our resources can provide. In Jesus' name. Amen.

COMMISSION AND BLESSING

You are sent out with authority
to proclaim good news and overcome evil.
God has blessed us in Christ
with every spiritual blessing.
Take nothing for your journey,
but travel light, depending on God.
God goes with us in all we do
and is present wherever we dwell.
If people turn away from your witness,
do not despair, but continue in ministry.
We will shake the dust off our feet
and announce again the grace of God.
Amen. **Amen.**

(See hymn No. 60.)

Pentecost 9
(July 17–23)

Old Testament: 2 Samuel 11:1–15
Psalm 53
Epistle: Ephesians 2:11–22
Gospel: Mark 6:30–34

CALL TO WORSHIP
Come, workers of evil and seekers for truth.
Come, all who are corrupt and all faithful ones.
Sometimes we say, "There is no God";
for God seems absent and unfeeling.
Come apart for a time to rest and reflect;
bring the hopes that survive God's silences.
Through Christ, we are no longer strangers
who call on God in doubt and terror.
Come from far and near, from trust and fears,
that you may be a dwelling place for the Spirit.
We are full citizens with the saints of God,
members of God's own household.

INVOCATION
God, whom we know through deeds of love and wrath, whom we worship and ignore, look on us today. Break through our schemes and our plotting to bring wisdom and perspective to our thoughts and our tasks. Bring us near to the Source of our being and hold us accountable for the choices we make. Amen.

CALL TO CONFESSION
From the midst of temptations not resisted and pretenses not denied, let us gather to tear down the walls between ourselves and God. They are of our own making, but we need help to dismantle them. Come now with honest talk and open thoughts to clear away sin's debris.

PRAYER OF CONFESSION
O God, how can we give up the sin that reshapes the world to our advantage, or turn away from the lust that destroys all sense of value? We confess to evil selfishness and bloody hostility. We eat up people as if they were bread, and turn away from the healing waters of divine love as if they hold no worth for us. Forgive us, God. The pain of our corruption and depravity is too great to bear. Create in us a new humanity, reconciled by the cross of Christ. Amen.

ASSURANCE OF FORGIVENESS

All who were once far off are being brought near in the blood of Christ; our hostility is overcome and our sins are truly forgiven. Rise up to make peace with all whom you meet. God is creating a new humanity among us. Amen.

COLLECT

May we be reached by what we require most from your word, O God. If we need reassurance, help us to hear it. If our actions condemn us, prompt us to face the evil within that leads to hostile acts. Whatever our need, speak to us in ways we can understand, and move us toward a just response. Amen.

OFFERTORY INVITATION

We are powerful people who have learned to grab for what we want. What if we were to give with the same intensity? We covet for ourselves what others have. What would happen if we were as passionate about sharing? What does the Shepherd expect us to give today?

OFFERTORY PRAYER

Again and again, O God, you have restored our fortune. Even when we have little, there is enough; and when we share, the blessings multiply. Thank you for treating us with compassion and granting us the honor of serving as your stewards. May these gifts proclaim your peace. Amen.

COMMISSION AND BLESSING

You are no longer strangers to God's covenant,
for you are citizens and saints.
    We are God's holy temple,
    a dwelling place of the Spirit.
God is creating a new humanity,
and uniting us with one another.
    We will be peacemakers where we are
    and wherever our influence can reach.
Go in peace, with joy and gladness,
for God will grant understanding and strength.
    We rejoice in our ministry
    and claim our citizenship in God's realm.
Amen.   **Amen.**

(See hymns No. 61 and No. 62.)

Pentecost 10
(July 24–30)

Old Testament: 2 Samuel 12:1–14
Psalm 32
Epistle: Ephesians 3:14–21
Gospel: John 6:1–15

CALL TO WORSHIP

Be glad in God, and rejoice, O righteous;
shout for joy, all upright of heart.
God has called us by name
and poured out abundant mercy upon us.
God has multiplied our resources
and blessed us with food for body and soul.
Christ dwells in our hearts through faith
that we may be rooted and grounded in love.
God grants us power to comprehend
love's breadth and length, its heights and depths.
The love of Christ surpasses knowledge
and fills us with the fullness of God.

INVOCATION

Great God, whose glory is beyond the reach of our imagination, and whose response to us is more generous than we can ask or think, deliver us from the limitations we impose on our own humanity. Your hand is heavy on us in our deceits. You call us from our hiding places to find refuge and strength in you. You summon us from our self-interest to share what we have, that all your people may eat. Help us to hear you in this hour, that we may respond every day to your will. Amen.

CALL TO CONFESSION

Let us bow our knees before God, who understands us as we are, yet is always ready to help us become all we are intended to be. Let us never seek to hide the guilt we know or to perpetuate the blindness that keeps us from realizing the full extent of our sin. Let us pray.

PRAYER OF CONFESSION

O God, we deserve to die, for we have accepted what belongs to others as our own—their substance, their time, their lives, poured out for our comfort, and to protect us. We have deceived ourselves, denying our guilt and turning away from the haunting indictment, "You are the one!" We have sinned; our transgressions immerse us in guilt from which we cannot cleanse ourselves. O God, hear our prayer and accomplish within us what we cannot do. Wipe away the devastation of our broken community and lift from us the load of guilt too heavy for us to bear. Unless you forgive, we cannot stand. Amen.

ASSURANCE OF FORGIVENESS

Blessed are those whose transgressions are forgiven, whose sins are covered. When we let go of our deceits, God raises us from our iniquities and frees us from the burden of our misdirected loyalties. Surely God has put away our sin; we shall not die, but shall live as God's own, forgiven, preserved, and delivered, in steadfast love. Amen.

COLLECT

By the riches of your glory, strengthen us. By the power of your word and work, transform us. By the wisdom of your counsel, teach us. Direct our thoughts and actions, O God, lest our eyes deceive us and immediate self-interest betray. Be our Deliverer, surrounding us with love that is eternal and joy that is complete. We pray in Jesus' name. Amen.

OFFERTORY INVITATION

Let us examine once more what we are prepared to give in response to Christ's invitation. To the hungry of the world, Jesus says, "Come and eat!" From the rich, the Savior requires the loaves and fish set aside for their own use. We are the rich; what will we share?

OFFERTORY PRAYER

What a joyous privilege you have given us, O God, to move from fearful withholding to giving with abandon and trust. Thank you for overcoming our doubts and selfishness so we can know the uplift of sharing. Sustain us by that food which prepares us for full participation in the realm of heaven, beginning here and now. Amen.

COMMISSION AND BLESSING

Be glad in God and rejoice, O righteous.
Carry forth your joyous songs, O upright of heart.
Our eyes have been opened
and we have been forgiven.
Know the love of Christ, surpassing all knowledge,
and the fullness of God, poured out in power.
Our ears have heard good news
of forgiveness and steadfast love.
May the riches of God's glory strengthen you within,
as Christ dwells in your hearts through faith.
To the One who is able to do more than we know
be glory in the church for generations to come.
Amen.   **Amen.**

(See hymn No. 63.)

Pentecost 11
(July 31–August 6)

Old Testament: 2 Samuel 12:15b–24
Psalm 34:11–22
Epistle: Ephesians 4:1–6
Gospel: John 6:24–35

CALL TO WORSHIP

Come, children of the Creator,
to learn the fear of God,
We bow in awe before Divine Majesty
and cry out for God's help.
God is near to the brokenhearted
and saves the crushed in spirit.
God hears us when we call
and delivers us from our troubles.
Many are the afflictions of the righteous,
but God delivers them from their pain.
God redeems our lives and gives them purpose.
God is with us in this time and place.

INVOCATION

Feed us, O God, in this time we spend together, with bread that is eternal. Unite us in a faithful response to your saving activity through Jesus Christ. Open us now to hear and experience, deep within, the word you intend for each one of us. Amen.

CALL TO CONFESSION

There is a moral structure to God's creation that we ignore at our peril. Yet we often choose to live as if the only standard that counts with us is our own immediate desires. So we violate God's purposes, the rights of other people, and our own integrity. Now is the time to examine ourselves and to confess all that separates us from the intentions of our Creator. Let us pray, first in individual silence and then in corporate confession.

PRAYER OF CONFESSION

O God, when we let you touch the deep places within us we are moved to tears of remorse. Again and again we violate the best you intend for us, to pursue our own whims and desires. We labor for food that perishes and ignore the Bread of Life. We take for ourselves what you intend for others, and resent your questioning of our stewardship. We settle for fragmentation rather than working for unity. O God, forgive and heal and empower us, we pray. Amen.

ASSURANCE OF FORGIVENESS

The face of God is turned against evildoers; they are cut off from remembrance. Yet those who take refuge in God will not be condemned. God hears our cries and lifts us up from our troubles. God offers living water and food that endure to eternal life. Let us receive God's gracious gift of forgiveness with joy and renewed commitment. Amen.

COLLECT

We seek Jesus. Reveal to us that Living Presence who brought change and vision to people who were hungry. Fill us with hunger for your truth, that we may be filled with the bread of eternity. Unite us in one body, one spirit, one hope, that we may participate fully in the life you intend for us. Amen.

OFFERTORY INVITATION

As we have been fed, we are sent to feed others. Whatever their need, we know the source of food to nourish them. God supplies the resources we have to give. Let us participate in God's redeeming activity through our offerings of self and substance.

OFFERTORY PRAYER

May our gifts be a worthy response to your call, and our service be a faithful reply to the love we have known in Christ. May these offerings and our lives be poured out in all lowliness, meekness, and patience to communicate your love and your peace. Amen.

COMMISSION AND BLESSING

You have been fed by the Spirit;
Walk, now, where the Spirit leads.
> **We are eager to maintain the unity of the Spirit
> in the bond of peace.**
We are united in hope
and are sent out to share that hope.
> **We will labor for things of lasting value
> rather than focus on what is perishable.**
Love one another, with patience and trust,
and enjoy together the goodness of life.
> **God provides all that we need for life;
> we shall feast on the manna from heaven.**
Amen.   **Amen.**

(See hymn No. 64.)

Pentecost 12
(August 7–13)

Old Testament: 2 Samuel 14:4–17 (alt.)
2 Samuel 18:1, 5, 9–15
Psalm 143:1–8
Epistle: Ephesians 4:25—5:2
Gospel: John 6:35, 41–51
John 8:2–11 (alt.)

CALL TO WORSHIP

Come, believing in one who relieves your thirst
and feeds your hunger with living bread.
Christ is the bread of life,
who draws us into God's presence.
It is frightening to stand before our Creator,
before the Sovereign Ruler of the Universe.
God knows everything we do
and is aware of all our thoughts.
Those who trust God shall know life eternal,
even in the midst of this world.
The Holy Spirit moves among us and within,
teaching us the way we should go.

INVOCATION

Hear our prayers, O God, and give ear to our supplications. In your
faithfulness and righteousness make response to our cries. We have been
pursued by our enemies, outside us and within, until we feel crushed by
life. Shadows overwhelm us and our spirits grow faint. Do not hide your
face from us, lest we sink deeper in agony and despair. Let us hear, early
in the morning, your steadfast love and find assurance to meet the day.
Amen.

CALL TO CONFESSION

Again and again we assault God's design for human society with our own
self-centered schemes. We lie and cheat and steal, without recognizing
that we do so. We grieve the Holy Spirit with clamorous speech and
vindictive actions that we seek to justify. We need to repent and realize
forgiveness, for we cannot turn away from evil without God's help.

PRAYER OF CONFESSION

O Sovereign God, we confess that our plans for ourselves ignore the
needs of many of our sisters and brothers. We try to shut out the larger

world that does not fit our comfortable design. We are angry when called to account, and bitter when circumstances do not work out to our advantage. We are quick to see the sins of others and slow to recognize our own. Keep us from throwing stones, O God, and protect us from the missiles others would throw at us. Forgive our preoccupation with minor concerns in the midst of major problems. Lead us, so we may imitate your ways and walk in your love. Through Christ. Amen.

ASSURANCE OF FORGIVENESS

God does not condemn us, but meets us in Jesus Christ with the word: Go, and do not sin again. Whoever believes has eternal life. God does not wish to destroy us, but to lead us to fullness of life. Meditate on what God has done and be glad. Realize anew all that links you to God and humanity, and find renewed wholeness. Forgive one another as God has forgiven you. Amen.

COLLECT

God of the bitter and the tenderhearted, open to us your word of life that we may see and understand ourselves in the stories of your children long ago. Save us from the judgment we deserve, and feed us with the Bread of Life. Let us hear again of your steadfast love, for we put our trust in you. Amen.

OFFERTORY INVITATION

Wonder again at all that God's hands have wrought. All the work of our hands uses resources we cannot create. For the privilege of using them, we give thanks as we reinvest a portion in our shared ministry and mission. Let us bring our offerings with joy.

OFFERTORY PRAYER

As recipients of the bread of life, we offer bread to the hungry. For the gift of living water, we reach out to those who are thirsty. In the name of One who shared our flesh and put life itself on the line for justice and truth, we gladly dedicate our time, talents, and treasure. Draw us near to you, as we imitate your generosity. Amen.

COMMISSION AND BLESSING

Depart to serve the One who relieves your thirst
and feeds your hunger with living bread.
  Christ, the Bread of Life, sends us forth
  to live by God's purposes in the world.
Our Creator goes with us, wherever we go;
how awesome it is to journey with God!
  We long to be honest in all we say and do
  and to reflect God's love and care everywhere.
God blesses us with eternal life here and now
and empowers our service as beloved children.

We will walk in love, serving in Christ's name,
forgiving others as we have been forgiven.
Amen. **Amen.**

(See hymns No. 65 and No. 66.)

Pentecost 13
(August 14–20)

Old Testament: 2 Samuel 18:24–33
Psalm 102:1–12
Epistle: Ephesians 5:15–20
Gospel: John 6:51–58

CALL TO WORSHIP
Our days pass away like smoke;
who will note our presence?
Hear our prayers, O God;
let our cries come before you.
We eat ashes like bread;
who will fill the emptiness within?
Do not hide your face from us, O God,
as we call out to you in our distress.
From sleepless nights and anguished days,
we come together to seek God's help.
Incline your ear to us, O God,
and answer speedily when we call.

INVOCATION
Hear us, O God, in our losses and in our grief. Come to us when our pain
seems too grievous to bear. In the midst of our foolishness lead us to know
your will. When we misuse your gifts, may your anger bring us to
awareness of our responsibility. Move among us, that we may worship in
spirit and in truth. Amen.

CALL TO CONFESSION
It is not easy to face our sin or to admit that we are less than we pretend to
be. We find it easier to raise protective barriers than to break down our
defenses and allow God to change us. Share now in the power of honest
confession.

PRAYER OF CONFESSION
Great God, we confess that we have walked in our own way, wasting our
days in trivial pursuits and destroying the precious gifts you have en-

trusted to us. We have grasped for bread that does not satisfy and turned away from living water that brings life. Our worst enemies are within us. Deliver us, we pray, from your indignation and anger as we seek new ways to relate to you and one another. Amen.

ASSURANCE OF FORGIVENESS

God hears our cries and weeps with us. God wills the best for us in all circumstances and works with us to overcome the unbearable. As we walk with Christ, God promises to abide with us and raise us up. Let us live no longer in our distress and loneliness, but accept the gifts of God. Amen.

COLLECT

May your word feed us in all our times of loss, loneliness, and fear. May we partake of the Bread of Life to our eternal blessing. So fill us with your Spirit that our lives may break into songs of praise. Teach us in all circumstances to give thanks. Amen.

OFFERTORY INVITATION

God's gifts to the world are sometimes sent through us. We are a channel or a barrier between God and those persons with whom we share our days. What will you give today to increase the flow of good news among us and into a needy world?

OFFERTORY PRAYER

Accept our offerings of self and substance to accomplish what we cannot do by ourselves. So link us with one another in hymns of faith that we may be a powerful influence for the good you want to accomplish through us. May all our gifts and our time be devoted to your Sovereign will. In Jesus' name. Amen.

COMMISSION AND BLESSING

Always, and for everything, give thanks.
Make melody to God with your whole heart.
We rejoice in the gift of God's spirit
as we go out to walk life's pathways.
Look carefully where you walk
and make wise use of your time.
We look to Christ to deliver us from foolishness
and write a new melody on our hearts.
The Living God sends us forth to serve,
assuring us that we will find life.
Day by day we will feed on God's word
and moment by moment follow in Christ's way.
Amen.   **Amen.**

(See hymn No. 67.)

Pentecost 14
(August 21–27)

Old Testament: 2 Samuel 23:1–7
　　　　　　　Psalm 67
Epistle: Ephesians 6:1–4 (substitute lection)
Gospel: John 6:55–69

CALL TO WORSHIP

Come to the One who grants us eternal life;
gather in the name of Christ, who offers bread.
God has made with us an everlasting covenant
and prospered us in all the works of our hands.
Let us praise God, all people of faith,
for God has richly blessed us in all things.
God's ways are known in all the earth,
God's saving power among all nations.
God dawns on us like the morning light,
like sun flowing forth on a cloudless morning.
God sends the rain that waters the earth;
God rules justly over all creation.

INVOCATION

Speak to us, Spirit of God, as we are open to one another and to you.
Make your face to shine on us, and increase our joy in serving you. Keep
us from words and actions that hurt and destroy. May we honor and
respect one another, as you have graciously blessed us. Amen.

CALL TO CONFESSION

Let all who fear God pause to consider their covenant with the Creator
and their relationship with persons God has given us to love. We are
called to rule justly, share generously, and serve cheerfully. Let us
recognize together how we have been unsuccessful in our attempts to live
by God's intent.

PRAYER OF CONFESSION

Covenanting God, we confess that we have failed to speak and act
according to your purposes. We have bristled with thorns that keep
others at a distance. We provoke our children to anger and fail to honor
our parents. We accept your bread as our due, even as we distance
ourselves from true discipleship. Forgive us, we pray, that we may not be
consumed by the fire of your wrath. Amen.

ASSURANCE OF FORGIVENESS

God's saving power comes to us, and by God's grace we are forgiven. The Holy One offers eternal life to all who believe. Let us partake of the bread from heaven, offered for our continuing nourishment. Those who eat and drink what Christ offers will know that God abides in their midst and within each one. Amen.

COLLECT

Write your word on our tongues and our hearts, O God, even as we hear it with our ears. Speak to us once more, and touch us in ways we cannot avoid. Be gracious to us in our tentative groping for your truth and a faithful response. Amen.

OFFERTORY INVITATION

God has prospered us and blessed us, even when we have strayed from the guidance and instruction of our Sovereign. Let us praise God with gifts of thankfulness, and proclaim God's justice with sacrifice poured out for others.

OFFERTORY PRAYER

For the increase your earth has yielded, for the food your hand has provided, for the light of your presence that reveals meaning in our days, we give hearty thanks and praise. May our gifts honor all who have helped to make them possible, and assist many who need your good news in useful form. Grant us your Spirit as we give ourselves in your service. Amen.

COMMISSION AND BLESSING

Go forth to offer bread to the world
in the name of One who grants eternal life.
**We will seek to keep covenant
with the One who inspires all our efforts.**
Let all the earth know of God's way,
that people may recognize God's saving power.
**We will sing the praises of God
and proclaim God's blessing wherever we go.**
God will continue to send sunshine and rain,
that you may have food and drink in abundance.
**The Holy One goes with us day by day,
judging with equity and prospering our service.**
Amen.   **Amen.**

(See hymn No. 68.)

Pentecost 15
(August 28–September 3)

Old Testament: 1 Kings 2:1–4, 10–12
   Psalm 121
Epistle: Ephesians 6:10–20
Gospel: Mark 7:1–8, 14–15, 21–23

CALL TO WORSHIP

Gather, at God's command, to worship and pray,
to honor God with your whole being.
We I will lift up *our* my eyes to the hills.
   From whence does *our* my help come?
Our help comes from God,
who made heaven and earth.
   God is our keeper and protecter,
   shading us from the heat and storms of life.
The sun will not smite you by day
nor the moon by night.
   God will keep our lives from evil
   and be with us in all our coming and going.

INVOCATION

Sovereign God, whose commandments guide and teach, strengthen us today to live as you intend. Save us from the distractions of principalities and powers who rule this present age, and from spiritual hosts of wickedness that invade even the heavenly places. Hear the supplication of your saints wherever they gather, that your church may be filled with true ambassadors of the gospel. To that end, bless our worship. Amen.

CALL TO CONFESSION

We have come together, not because of our goodness, but out of awareness of our need. Our thinking is easily distorted to approve our own actions while we criticize the deeds of others. We need forgiveness in order to change our outlook and direction. Let us pray for new insight and healing.

PRAYER OF CONFESSION

Patient God, we come again to admit that we have honored you with our lips while our hearts were far away. We have taught doctrines from our own limited understanding, and held fast to our human traditions as if they embodied your will. We have filled our minds with evil thoughts that lead to destructive deeds. We are truly sorry for the many ways we have defiled your creation. We beg for your forgiveness and the opportunity for new beginnings. Amen.

ASSURANCE OF FORGIVENESS

The helmet of salvation is ours for the taking. God arms us for the spiritual battles we have yet to face, even as our past is forgiven. God will keep us from evil, confirm us in those testimonies by which we are called to live, and prosper us in all we do. Let us walk in faithfulness from this day forward. Amen.

COLLECT

Eternal God, who neither slumbers nor sleeps, awaken us now to the depths of truth to be found in the scriptures. Arm us once more to do battle with evil wherever we encounter it. Grant us discernment that we may hear, understand, and respond to your commands rather than cling to limited human precepts and traditions. Amen.

OFFERTORY INVITATION

We have prospered, not because we are deserving, but by God's generosity. Our worship is in vain if we do not acknowledge the source of all we have and all we are. It is God who has granted life and equipped us to fight its battles. Let us give thanks with our offerings.

OFFERTORY PRAYER

In faith and gratitude we return these gifts that they may proclaim the mystery of your love and glorify the gospel. May hearts and lives be drawn to you by the witness our offerings will make in this community of faith and among all people you call us to serve. In Jesus' name. Amen.

COMMISSION AND BLESSING

Be strong and courageous as you face this week.
Keep the charge of God and walk in God's ways.
**With all our heart and soul
we seek to walk in faithfulness all our days.**
As you face spiritual hosts of wickedness
put on the whole armor of God.
**We will gird ourselves with truth and righteousness,
with faith, salvation, and peace.**
God will guide and support you
as you give your best to hearing and serving.
**We will cherish and share the mystery of the gospel,
rededicating ourselves as ambassadors for Christ.**
Amen. Amen.
All: *Alleluia! Amen.*

(See hymn No. 69.)

Pentecost 16
(September 4–10)

Old Testament: Proverbs 2:1–8 (alt.)
                   Psalm 119:129–136
Epistle: James 1:17–27
Gospel: Mark 7:31–37

CALL TO WORSHIP

Incline your hearts to the wisdom of God;
seek integrity and understanding.
    The testimonies of God are wonderful;
    the unfolding of God's word gives light.
Receive God's word and treasure God's commandments;
cry out for insight and knowledge.
    Every good endowment and perfect gift
    is brought forth by the will of God.
Be quick to hear, slow to speak, slow to anger,
as doers of the word, not hearers only.
    We seek to be redeemed from human oppression
    to a faith that is pure and undefiled.

INVOCATION

Open our eyes so we may clearly see the wonders of your creation. Release our tongues to share the knowledge you impart. Transform our religion so its major focus is no longer on our own benefit, but on ministering to others as we have been blessed by you. Amen.

CALL TO CONFESSION

Cry out to God from the points of need you recognize in yourself. Seek understanding of the sin you do not comprehend. Let us together seek insight and forgiveness.

PRAYER OF CONFESSION

God of All Knowledge, Source of All Truth, we bring ourselves before you as we really are. We do not want to deceive ourselves, and we know we cannot deceive you. Let no iniquity have dominion over us. Redeem us from human oppression and the lure of distorted values. Silence the tongues that run wild with gossip and the ambitions that run roughshod over the aspirations of others. Open wellsprings of gratitude for your gifts we have taken for granted, and open our hearts to the needy people around us whom we have ignored. Then we can aspire to your forgiveness. Amen.

ASSURANCE OF FORGIVENESS

God grants wisdom and understanding to the upright and preserves the way of saints. When we turn to the Source of light, God's face shines on us and we experience the grace by which we live. God is a shield to all who walk in integrity and seek to keep themselves unstained from competing values of the world. Accept the gifts of God, and know you are forgiven. Amen.

COLLECT

We who were brought forth by your will, O God, seek again your word of truth. May we be attentive to your wisdom and open to new understandings. Sharpen our insight and deepen our commitment. Move us to be doers of the word, not hearers only. Amen.

OFFERTORY INVITATION

We who are the first fruits of God's love come now in gratitude to bring our best to extend the church's outreach and mission. We know it is not enough to share with one another the amazing good news we are discovering. Let us give generously and joyously, that the whole world may know God's love.

OFFERTORY PRAYER

Because you have called us to visit widows and orphans, we bring these offerings to serve you where we cannot go. We would bring all in need of healing to the feet of Jesus through gifts sent to minister in Christ's name. May we reach out to all impoverished spirits with renewed understanding and practical help. We dedicate ourselves, with these material tokens, that we may truly become doers of the word and not hearers only. Amen.

COMMISSION AND BLESSING

The hand of God has touched us,
and we have known forgiveness and healing.
> **We cannot help but share our experiences**
> **and proclaim the joy we are feeling.**
We have heard anew the testimony of God's word
and been moved to keep God's commandments.
> **We have received the insight we have sought.**
> **God's promises have steadied our footsteps.**
We have been empowered as doers of the word
and not hearers only. Let us act our faith!
> **We commit ourselves to walk with integrity**
> **in paths of justice, truth, and peace.**
Amen. **Amen.**

(See hymn No. 70.)

Pentecost 17
(September 11–17)

Old Testament: Proverbs 22:1–2, 8–9
Psalm 125
Epistle: James 2:1–5, 8–10, 14–17
Gospel: Mark 8:27–38

CALL TO WORSHIP

Listen to the whispers of God,
who calls us from work to times of worship.
We trust the ways of God
and respond to the Spirit moving among us.
God, who is Maker of all creation,
calls rich and poor to meet together.
All of us are worthy in God's sight,
and God's favor is meant for all to share.
Hear the good news of all God has given for us,
even the rejection and death of Jesus Christ.
In gratitude we deny ourselves, take up our cross,
and follow where Christ leads.

INVOCATION

All-knowing God, whose wisdom flies in the face of our own, open our
lives to your point of view. Teach us to pursue riches of the spirit more
than material gain. Enable us to value faithfulness more than safety and
security. Help us to stand with the poor and oppressed as advocates for
justice and equality, for we would follow Christ. Amen.

CALL TO CONFESSION

In Christ, we are called to declare our faith, to put into words and deeds
all that we truly believe. None of us has measured up to God's intention
for us, so we return once more to seek forgiveness and release from the
burden of guilt we carry. Let us pray.

PRAYER OF CONFESSION

O God, we are numbered among the evildoers who have turned aside
into crooked ways, wandering far from the paths on which you intend that
we go. We have chased after riches of silver and gold for ourselves, while
neglecting persons who are ill-clad and hungry. We have sown injustice
and reaped calamity, and then blamed you for deserting us. Forgive us,
Loving God, for permitting and pursuing evil and for showing partiality
to those most like ourselves. Save us from the guilt and pain we have

brought on our own lives and on your world. We pray in Jesus' name.
Amen.

ASSURANCE OF FORGIVENESS

We are convicted of our transgressions but also freed of them by God's
grace. We are guilty, but in facing that guilt, are forgiven. "The sceptor of
wickedness shall not rest upon the land allotted to the righteous." We are
liberated to live creatively and courageously, risking all that love of
neighbor requires. Amen.

COLLECT

O God, whose name is to be chosen above great riches, we trust in you.
Your love surrounds us like great mountains and your care fills the poor of
this world with hope. Lead us to discern your side in our present
circumstances, that we may have courage to serve with Christ, not
counting the cost. Amen.

OFFERTORY INVITATION

As long as sisters and brothers are ill-clad and hungry and we have more
than we need, it is our task to clothe and feed them. As long as some have
not heard the good news of God's love, we are called to share it. Let us
give with generous hearts.

OFFERTORY PRAYER

As we share our bread with the poor, open our ears and hearts to learn
from them to live by faith, not sight. Free us from our tendency to be
possessive and protective, that we may experience the freedom and joy of
giving. May faith and works together fill our lives with meaning and
purpose. In Jesus' name. Amen.

COMMISSION AND BLESSING

We have heard the whispers of God,
who sends us from our worship to serve our world.
We trust the ways of God
and respond to the Spirit's leading.
Abide in God and live by faith,
seeking not riches, but human community.
We seek to treat others as God's children
without partiality or distinction.
Because God has blessed us in Jesus Christ,
we are not afraid to take the risks of faith.
We are empowered to deny ourselves,
take up the cross and follow.
Amen.   **Amen.**

(See hymns No. 71 and No. 72.)

Pentecost 18
(September 18–24)

Old Testament: Job 28:20–28
Psalm 27:1–6
Epistle: James 3:13–18
Gospel: Mark 9:30–37

CALL TO WORSHIP

God is our light and our salvation;
whom shall we fear?
God is the stronghold of our lives;
of whom shall we be afraid?
Behold all the beauty of God
and make inquiry in God's temple.
We have come to worship and seek wisdom,
to find shelter and help amid life's storms.
God lifts us up from our doubts and fears,
granting us confidence and courage.
We will offer sacrifices of joy and thanksgiving,
we will sing and make melody to our God.

INVOCATION

Wise God, beyond our understanding, the whole creation looks to you for care. We are children of your creation, who need insight and empowerment. In these moments of worship, we bow in fear before your majesty and in trust before your peace. May worship restore us to our place in your plans. Amen.

CALL TO CONFESSION

Have we not placed ourselves in competition with others and turned away from community? Does ambition outrank mercy, and jealousy provide greater motivation than compassion? Surely we are in need of repentance and redirection. Let us approach the only source from which help may come.

PRAYER OF CONFESSION

Turn us away from evil thoughts and deeds, O God of Light and Salvation. Put down in us falsehood and boasting, jealousy and selfish ambition. We confess that we aspire to power and recognition, while you call us to service. We would like to be first, even when you counsel us to accept more humble roles. Grant us childlike trust and peaceable goals, as we seek to embody your purposes for us. Amen.

ASSURANCE OF FORGIVENESS

God understands and forgives. How shall we respond? God helps us to turn from evil and leave it behind us. Will we accept the beauty, mystery, and mercy with which God surrounds us? Receive the gifts of God for your continuing growth. Amen.

COLLECT

God of Wisdom, open to us your truth that we may bear good fruit and pursue peaceable goals. Keep us from jealousy and selfish ambition, from uncertainty and insincerity. May we be servants of your highest purposes. In Christ. Amen.

OFFERTORY INVITATION

What have you been discussing most along life's way? How have you invested the blessings God has poured into your life? Giving increases our joy, even as our gifts minister to the needs of many. You are invited to this ministry of sharing.

OFFERTORY PRAYER

We offer sacrifices of joy and thanksgiving, for you, God, have blessed us in mercy and wisdom, opening us to reason, gentleness, and purposeful service. May our work for you bear good fruits, and these offerings help to accomplish the tasks for which you have called us. Amen.

COMMISSION AND BLESSING

We have received wisdom from above;
let us carry it into our daily living.
  We go forth as servants of God,
  devoted to peace and righteousness.
Be peaceable, gentle, and open to reason,
full of mercy and good fruits.
  With sincerity and confidence
  we undertake the work to which God calls us.
Learn from children to honor God aright;
receive children as valuable expressions of God.
  The light of God's salvation shines on us.
  We go forth in the strength Christ gives.
Amen. **Amen.**

(See hymn No. 73.)

Pentecost 19
(September 25—October 1)

Old Testament: Job 42:1–6
  Psalm 27:7–14
Epistle: James 4:13–17; 5:7–11
Gospel: Mark 9:38–50

CALL TO WORSHIP

Happy are those who are steadfast in faith,
who show forth the mercy and compassion of God.
  God can do all things;
  no purpose of God can be thwarted.
In faith, we have uttered what we do not understand,
for the ways of God are too wonderful for us.
  We proclaim and question and even boast
  in our attempts to see and hear God at work.
We believe we will see God's goodness
and be led through pathways that bring life.
  We wait for God and the strength God offers,
  and our hearts take courage as we wait.

INVOCATION

O God, whom we have worshiped without knowing, show us who you
are. Hear us when we cry to you, for there is no one else to understand
our pain or to bear with us in our trials. Meet us here, amid our doubts
and questions, that we may know we are heard and understood. Amen.

CALL TO CONFESSION

Before the awesome majesty of the Eternal One, our thoughts and deeds
become millstones around our necks. Eyes and hands and feet have led us
from the ways of God. Yet our hearts say, we will seek God's face. Let us
pour out our sin before the One who offers forgiveness.

PRAYER OF CONFESSION

Compassionate and Merciful God, in our worst moments we despise
ourselves. We know what is right, but we fail to do it. We are easily
deceived by voices other than your own. When we seek your face our
vision is clouded by self-concern. When we intend to do your will, easier
paths beckon, and we follow them. Forgive us, God, as we repent in dust
and ashes. Save us from ourselves, that we may bear Christ's name with
renewed confidence. Amen.

ASSURANCE OF FORGIVENESS

God does not cast us off or forsake us. Our Creator does not give us up to the will of our adversaries. Mercy and forgiveness are offered us as gifts from God; let us receive them with joy and gratitude. Amen.

COLLECT

Open all our senses to encounter you through the pain and joy of human experience, recorded long ago. We wait for your coming in word and spirit, seeking not just to hear, but also to understand. Re-anchor the depths of our commitment and make us strong to withstand temptation. Grant us steadfastness and patience as we seek to serve you. Amen.

OFFERTORY INVITATION

Once again the opportunity is ours to proclaim the goodness of God through offering ourselves and the first fruits of our labors. May all that we give be a testimony to God's purposes among us.

OFFERTORY PRAYER

All that we give is first a gift from you, O God. It is a joy to invest in the mission of the church, both as a gathered community in this place and as a scattered people who day by day offer a cup of cold water in Christ's name to people who are thirsty. May our offerings help to reach where we ourselves cannot go. Amen.

COMMISSION AND BLESSING

Reach out with mercy and compassion
to the lonely, abused, and burdened.
God works out eternal purposes through us,
reaching out to those who despise themselves.
The God of our salvation will strengthen you
and grant courage for each day's tasks.
We have known the goodness of God
and rely on God's favor day by day.
Have salt in yourselves
and be at peace with one another.
The love of God keeps us steadfast,
and we find our happiness in helping others.
Amen.   **Amen.**

(See hymn No. 74.)

Pentecost 20
(October 2–8)

Old Testament: Genesis 2:18–24
Psalm 128
Epistle: Hebrews 1:1–4; 2:9–11
Gospel: Mark 10:2–16

CALL TO WORSHIP

God, by whom all things exist,
brings many to glory.
Blessed is everyone who fears God
and walks in God's ways.
God spoke in many ways to our ancestors,
by prophets, apostles, and martyrs.
God has spoken most clearly in Jesus Christ,
the pioneer of our salvation.
Jesus welcomed persons of all ages
and gave special recognition to children.
We come expectantly to learn of God's realm
and to know the love of God poured out in Christ.

INVOCATION

Loving God, who created us to live in families and to realize human community in the church of Jesus Christ, help us today. You have granted us prosperity and many opportunities for happiness. We have been blessed as were the children whom Jesus welcomed and embraced. In Christ we recognize our origins and seek to live as your children and as brothers and sisters to one another. Amen.

CALL TO CONFESSION

When we recognize the greatness and glory of God we are moved to repent of misdeeds and broken relationships. In the light of God's love we reach to become more fully what God intends for us to be and to do. Let us seek forgiveness and reconciliation.

PRAYER OF CONFESSION

O God, you have made us for human companionship, but we have chosen our own lonely way. You have called us to make commitments and to live by them, but we have violated our promises and made excuses for ourselves. You have created us to reflect your glory, but we have turned away from the example and sacrifice of Christ to seek our own way. Turn us back from our limited vision and hardness of heart to become more fully your own people. Amen.

ASSURANCE OF FORGIVENESS

Blessed is everyone who fears God and walks in God's ways. By the grace of God, Jesus tasted death for everyone and triumphed over it so we can experience newness of life. Praise God! Amen.

COLLECT

Gracious God, you provide the fruit of our labor and the opportunity for meaningful relationships. Speak to us now as you spoke to our ancestors. Confront us with the living Christ that our lives may be touched and transformed. Amen.

OFFERTORY INVITATION

All of us, and all we own, come from God. Our offerings are a measure of our gratitude. Let us give thanks as we dedicate our offerings and ourselves to God's service.

OFFERTORY PRAYER

In grateful appreciation of the gift of life and all that adds to our enjoyment of that gift, we dedicate these offerings to proclaim your good news. As sisters and brothers of Jesus Christ, we recognize the whole human family as bone of our bones and flesh of our flesh. We want for them all that we appreciate in our own lives. May these offerings help to unite us in your service. Amen.

COMMISSION AND BLESSING

Depart from old dependencies and securities
to take the risks of commitment and faithfulness.
> **God calls us to lives of response and responsibility,**
> **yet with the openness and spontaneity of a child.**

Let God melt the hardness of your hearts
and penetrate the rigid prejudices of your lives.
> **We will listen for the promptings of God**
> **in our meditation and our decision-making.**

God in Christ welcomes you
to life with eternity in it.
> **We feel the touch of God's Spirit**
> **and feel welcomed to the realm of God.**

Amen.   **Amen.**

(See hymn No. 75.)

Pentecost 21
(October 9–15)

Old Testament: Genesis 3:8–19
Psalm 90:1–12
Epistle: Hebrews 4:1–3, 9–13
Gospel: Mark 10:17–30

CALL TO WORSHIP

God calls, "Where are you?"
and we respond with guilty silences.
God calls, and we are afraid;
God is our dwelling place, and we try to move out.
In Christ, God summons us back
to full participation in life.
It is hard to reorder our priorities
to give God first place in our lives.
There is good news here of sabbath rest
and resources to meet all life's troubles.
We come to listen for God's active, living word,
and open ourselves to the One who knows us best.

INVOCATION

Powerful God, before whom all human history is but a breath, turn us from our petty concerns to seek eternal values. Grant us hearts of wisdom that our days may be lived to their fullest. Ground us in your commandments and then free us to follow where Christ leads. Amen.

CALL TO CONFESSION

God asks us, "What have you done?" and in the light of God's countenance our secret sins are revealed. Let us examine ourselves and seek forgiveness, lest we miss God's possibilities.

PRAYER OF CONFESSION

Amid the toil and troubles of life, we admit, O God, that we focus too much on ourselves and the things we can accumulate. We fail to see the pain of others, and if we do see their agony, we discount it. We blame others for the mistakes we ourselves make, and expect special consideration when we are disobedient. If we are faithful to your commands, we turn away dismayed when more is expected of us. Save us, God, from this way of death. Amen.

ASSURANCE OF FORGIVENESS

All who put God's will first in their lives will know that God can accomplish what is impossible by our own efforts. We will know, even when life is difficult, that salvation has come and eternal life is a reality. Praise God! Amen.

COLLECT

Walk among us, God, with mercy and not wrath. Help us to hear your good news and make faithful response. May your word cut through our pretenses and purify our hearts. Refocus our attention from material abundance we can accumulate to the riches of right relationships. In Jesus' name. Amen.

OFFERTORY INVITATION

Jesus said to one who trusted in his own goodness, "Go, sell what you have, and give to the poor, . . . come, follow me." That invitation is also for us. May we not turn away sorrowfully, but welcome the joy of sharing.

OFFERTORY PRAYER

God of High Expectations, lift us from our limited views of faithfulness. Free us from our dependence on things so we can move from living protectively to sharing without counting the cost. May we give, not for rewards, but in joyous thankfulness. Amen.

COMMISSION AND BLESSING

We cannot truly worship and not be changed;
so we leave one another now to face new ventures.
  God has walked among us to reveal us to ourselves;
  God has spoken and acted to save us.
Our lives have been opened to new possibilities
and we have been challenged in unexpected ways.
  God's anger is as real as God's mercy,
  and we know we cannot avoid God's judgment.
God promises eternal life as a gift,
not as a status we can earn.
  With God all things are possible;
  we rejoice in the goodness of God.
Amen.   **Amen.**

(See hymns No. 76 and 77.)

Pentecost 22
(October 16–22)

Old Testament: Isaiah 53:7–12
Psalm 35:17–28
Epistle: Hebrews 4:14–16
Gospel: Mark 10:35–45

CALL TO WORSHIP

With confidence, draw near to the throne of grace
to find mercy and help in times of need.
We bring our burdens and cares,
hoping to find relief and renewed strength.
Give thanks for God's presence
in all times and places.
We rejoice that God hears us
in this time and place.
Before God, nothing can be hidden;
no thought or deed escapes God's notice.
We come to face ourselves as we really are,
aspiring to become all God wants us to be.

INVOCATION

Righteous God, before whom deceit can bring only judgment, we would
not cut ourselves off from you or seek to present ourselves falsely. Help us
to see ourselves as you see us, to rejoice in the strength you supply, and
to face the weaknesses you can help us overcome. In Jesus' name. Amen.

CALL TO CONFESSION

Come, all who seek to rule over one another, for it shall not be so among
you. Come, all who are weak and tempted, for Christ knows the trials you
face and has triumphed over them. Bring your sin before God, that a right
relationship may be restored.

PRAYER OF CONFESSION

Eternal God, we confess that we have yielded to temptation and violated
your intentions for us. By our actions we have invited some of the
calamities that befall us. By our inaction for good we have allowed evil to
triumph. Some people are wrongfully our foes; some are victims of our
deceit or prejudice. Rescue us, O God, from all that breaks right relationships with one another, with you, and with our own best selves.
Amen.

ASSURANCE OF FORGIVENESS

Jesus Christ was numbered among the transgressors to bear our sins, pouring out life and facing death on our behalf, that we might be accounted righteous. Praise God for the saving activity of the Human One, who came not to be served, but to give up life as a ransom for many. Amen.

COLLECT

Move us, O God, toward a commitment able to withstand the baptism of fire and the cup of bitter suffering. Break your silence to speak to us now as you spoke to prophets of old. Stimulate our thanksgiving for the selfless sacrifice of Jesus Christ on our behalf. Amen.

OFFERTORY INVITATION

Jesus gave life itself as an offering for our sin. What shall we give in thanksgiving for life and salvation? Let us worship our Creator with our gifts and through lives invested in service to God and one another.

OFFERTORY PRAYER

May your will be realized through these gifts, dedicated to your service, O God. May the act of giving strengthen our commitment to the causes for which Christ died and involve us in the acts of compassion by which Christ lived. May all we say and do work to accomplish your peace. Amen.

COMMISSION AND BLESSING

The grace of God goes with us,
and God's mercy meets us in times of need.
We leave behind our burdens and cares
to face life's challenges with renewed strength.
God's presence does not change our circumstances,
but we are changed to meet their challenge.
We rejoice that God hears us and responds;
God is available when we call.
Go forth to work for the good of all God's creatures
in selfless devotion to the will of God.
May God's work prosper at our hands
and the peace of God transform us all.
Amen.   **Amen.**

(See hymn No. 78.)

Pentecost 23
(October 23–29)

Old Testament: Jeremiah 31:7–9
Psalm 126
Epistle: Hebrews 5:1–6
Gospel: Mark 10:46–52.

CALL TO WORSHIP
Arise, take heart, Jesus is calling you;
respond to Christ's summons with joy.
We hear God calling us by name,
to lead us by the Spirit in new paths.
God gathers us from all the earth
and from every human need.
We come for healing and consolation
and to offer our joyous thanksgiving.
God leads us by refreshing waters,
and keeps our feet from stumbling.
We who have sown in tears
will reap with shouts of joy.

INVOCATION
God of all peoples, may we be your people in all our thoughts and actions. We are your wayward children, returning to find rest and renewal. We are also disciples of Christ, eager for new insights and firm direction. Fill us now with the warmth of your presence that we may find new joy in your service. Amen.

CALL TO CONFESSION
Come to the One who promises to deal gently with the ignorant and the wayward. Come, all who are beset with weaknesses, to the One who promises to make us strong. Let us seek God's mercy and forgiveness.

PRAYER OF CONFESSION
Accepting God, we admit that our sins have created barriers we cannot surmount. Our waywardness has brought us troubles with which we find it hard to deal. Calamities we feel we do not deserve have left us paralyzed and unable to see the good you intend for us. Help us throw off mantles of depression and self-concern as we know once more your healing touch. Amen.

ASSURANCE OF FORGIVENESS

"Go your way; your faith has made you well." Pain cannot have the last word, nor can loss weigh us down forever. God restores our fortunes and does great things for us. Our mouths are filled with laughter, and our tongues move with shouts of joy. Thanks be to God! Amen.

COLLECT

Open our eyes to receive new sight, our ears to hear your sounds of joy, our hearts to feel the warmth of Christ's compassion and self-giving. Reveal to us our priesthood, under Christ, and equip us to follow where Christ leads. Amen.

OFFERTORY INVITATION

God has done great things for us, restoring our fortunes when we lose faith in ourselves and reassuring us of the goodness God intends. Let us respond in joyous generosity to the blessings God bestows.

OFFERTORY PRAYER

Thank you, God, for the joy of receiving and giving. Thank you for saving and healing us, for relieving our pain and strengthening us in times of loss. Accept these gifts of gratitude as we invest them in the lives of people. May others know the joy we find in serving you. In Jesus' name. Amen.

COMMISSION AND BLESSING

Your faith has made you well;
depart in joy and peace.
> **Our burdens have been lightened
> and our hope is renewed.**
God sends you out to all the earth
to minister to every human need.
> **God has equipped us to serve where we are,
> and to reach out in new ways.**
Live out your priesthood under the Great High Priest;
follow Christ's lead, inviting others to faith.
> **May our joy and laughter, our love and trust,
> attract others to the good news of the gospel.**
Amen.   **Amen.**

(See hymn No. 79.)

Pentecost 24
(October 30–November 5)

Old Testament: Deuteronomy 6:1–9
Psalm 119:33–48
Epistle: Hebrews 7:23–28
Gospel: Mark 12:28–34

CALL TO WORSHIP

Hear, all people, the Sovereign One is God;
whose commandments and promises are sure,
Teach us your statutes, O God,
and grant understanding that we may keep them.
You shall love God with all your heart,
with all your soul, mind, and strength.
We love in response to God's steadfast love
and rejoice in the salvation Christ offers.
God's love prompts us to love ourselves aright
and to love our neighbor as ourselves.
We will write these laws on our hearts
and teach them to our children.

INVOCATION

Teach us, O God, to delight in your commandments and to meditate on
your statutes. We draw near in the name of our great High Priest, seeking
to know as we are known. Grant us life in your righteousness, and trust
based on your word. May this hour of worship be a time of growth. Amen.

CALL TO CONFESSION

Christ has called us to love God with our whole being, to love ourselves as
we are loved by God, and to love our neighbor as ourselves. We, who fail
to make these our first priority, are invited to confess our neglect and
seek empowerment to live more faithfully.

PRAYER OF CONFESSION

Turn us, O God, from our vanities so we may value the gifts you have
given and number ourselves among your children. We confess that we
have nursed our egos in ways that are destructive and judged others
rather than loving them. We live moment by moment as if there were no
eternal verities, and deny your presence by our inattention. Forgive us,
O God, and call us back to your ways. Amen.

ASSURANCE OF FORGIVENESS

God's promises are confirmed for those in awe of their Creator. God turns away the reproach we dread and frees us to walk once more as people liberated by a word of grace. When we are truly sorry for our sin and resolve to walk in love of God and neighbor, we hear once more, "You are not far from the realm of God." Amen.

COLLECT

Sharpen our hearing and incline our hearts to your testimony, that we may receive the wholeness you offer in a land flowing with milk and honey. May our hearing lead to knowing, and knowing prompt our doing. In the name of Jesus Christ, holy, blameless, and unstained, who offered up self for us in a sacrifice we can only embrace but never repeat. Amen.

OFFERTORY INVITATION

What shall we offer in thanksgiving for Christ's sacrifice, and how will we return the love poured out on our behalf? Surely love of God and neighbor prompts our generous response. Let us answer God's abundant provision for us through joyous sharing.

OFFERTORY PRAYER

May your word of truth be in our mouths, even as these gifts give expression to those who will carry it around the world. Confirm your promises for more and more of your children as we learn to share the abundance you entrust to us. May your love and ours go with every gift. Amen.

COMMISSION AND BLESSING

Once more we have heard God's commandments
and witnessed promises that are sure.
We have listened to God, teaching us to love,
and have learned anew the depth of God's care.
Love God with all your heart, soul, and might,
and love your neighbor as yourself.
The whole of God's law is in these verses;
we long to make them real in our lives.
God writes these laws on our hearts
and grants us power to keep them.
We will carry them with us
and will teach them to our children.
Amen.   **Amen.**

(See hymn No. 80.)

Pentecost 25
(November 6–12)

Old Testament: 1 Kings 17:8–16
Psalm 146
Epistle: Hebrews 9:24–28
Gospel: Mark 12:38–44

CALL TO WORSHIP

Come, travelers and sojourners;
there is a place for you here.
God grants bread for our journey
and offers places of refuge on the way.
Praise God, who offers justice for the oppressed
and opens the eyes of the blind.
God brings our wickedness to ruin ·
and rejects our blind pursuit of riches.
Happy are those who hope in God,
and avail themselves of God's ever-present help.
God reigns in righteousness forever and ever;
we will sing God's praises as long as we live!

INVOCATION

Attune us in this sanctuary to the reality of Christ's eternal reign. May
your presence be so real to us that our lives are brought into harmony
with your aims for justice and peace. Make us instruments of your help
and carriers of your hope, both in this place and as we go our separate
ways. Amen.

CALL TO CONFESSION

God's help is as near as our requests, as dependable as the breath of life
that God has given. Surrounded by the gifts of God, we often take them
for granted. Let us take time to recognize and admit our wayward pursuit
of goals that are not God's.

PRAYER OF CONFESSION

We confess, O God, that we put our trust in things we can see. We pursue
human schemes because your will seems so illusive. When we discern
what you intend it seems too demanding. We vie for recognition and
honors without realizing the effect of our actions on others. We beg to be
freed from the tyranny of our own ambitions to serve where we are. In
Jesus' name. Amen.

ASSURANCE OF FORGIVENESS

In Christ you are offered a new design for living; receive it. Give what you have, without counting the cost. Keep the faith by giving it away. Accept Christ's sacrifice on your behalf, that sin may cease to dominate your life. Amen.

COLLECT

Show us your miracles in the midst of each day. Appear to us once more, for we eagerly await your word. Keep faith with us when our lack of faith sends us reeling through life without purpose or direction. Amen.

OFFERTORY INVITATION

It is not the size of our gift, but the sincerity of our commitment that counts with God. We are called to give in proportion to our blessings, as an act of dedication to our God.

OFFERTORY PRAYER

We dare to give because all we have has been given to us. Even when we have little, we know ourselves richly blessed. We bring these offerings on behalf of those who hunger, those who seek freedom and justice, those who long to see, and all who have no hope. Help us to accomplish your purposes where we live and work. Amen.

COMMISSION AND BLESSING

God loves the righteous and watches over sojourners;
depart in the assurance that God cares for you.
God's reign is just and endures forever;
God's purposes are being worked out, even now.
Trust the ways of God, not the schemes of human rulers;
happy are those whose help and hope is God.
God provides the courage to take risks
and the faith to go forward against great odds.
God upholds those who are vulnerable
and provides for all who are oppressed.
We will sing God's praise as long as we live;
God reigns in righteousness forever and ever.
Amen.   **Amen.**

(See hymn No. 81.)

Pentecost 26
(November 13–19)

Old Testament: Daniel 7:9–14
Psalm 145:8–13
Epistle: Hebrews 10:11–18
Gospel: Mark 13:24–32

CALL TO WORSHIP

God is present with us in all experiences of life
and hears our cries as we gather for worship.
Amid life's storms we see evidence of God's presence,
and deep within us we know God reigns.
God is gracious, faithful, and full of compassion,
offering mercy and forgiveness to all who seek it.
In the midst of calamity and tribulation
we look to God's rule, not to our own designs.
Praise God for the marvelous works of creation,
as we seek to participate in God's new day.
God's creative work continues among us,
as God's law is being written in our hearts.

INVOCATION

God of the Fire and Tumult, speak to us in our dark days, when the
heavens are shaken and our lives are in turmoil. Lift among us a vision of
your glory. Before your vast power over all the far reaches of time and
space, we bow in awe and reverence. Grant that this hour may turn our
thoughts and actions in new directions. Amen.

CALL TO CONFESSION

Come away from all evil that holds you in its grasp. Awaken to God's word
that convicts and challenges. Lay aside the burdens of your mistakes and
failures. Seek the cleansing power God's own messenger provides to
those who pray for pardon and deliverance.

PRAYER OF CONFESSION

O God, we are frightened when we step back to view our sin. We do not
understand how there could be so much evil in what we do and say. Your
way has been evident to us, but we have not followed it. The splendor of
your reign has been proclaimed, but we seek our own systems and
authorities. You have stayed with us, but we have tried to avoid you. Let
not the fires of your wrath consume us, or your judgment fall heavily on
our heads. Have compassion on us, in the name of Jesus Christ, whose
return to our lives we await with eager longing. Amen.

ASSURANCE OF FORGIVENESS

The sacrifice of Jesus Christ was the perfect offering, given to take away our sin. God forgives and forgets the wrong we have done and grants new opportunities for doing good. Join the multitudes who praise God without ceasing. Amen.

COLLECT

All-powerful God, whom words cannot describe or adequately address, move our imaginations as we listen for your word. Use the pictures of former years to expand our perceptions of your glory and power. Move us beyond narrow reasoning that our emotions may be engaged in the quest for your truth. Send your Holy Spirit to bear witness within and among us. Amen.

OFFERTORY INVITATION

The books of God are opened. The extent of our commitment is known. Our offerings are but a dim reflection of the total sacrifice of Christ on our behalf. Let not our response be a hollow mockery of that perfect gift.

OFFERTORY PRAYER

Receive our gifts with those of our sisters and brothers around the world, that all nations, languages, and peoples may unite in glorious anthems of praise and thanksgiving. Alert us all to everyday evidence of your presence and the splendor of your reign. Write your covenant on our minds and empower us to keep the promises we have made. Amen.

COMMISSION AND BLESSING

Carry the flame of God's love in Christ
into a world shaken by fear of impending doom.
We will not dwell in the shadows,
for the glory of Christ is coming to us.
Pass on to others the compassion you have received;
share with them your experience of God's presence.
We will give thanks for God's faithfulness
and live out our gratitude day by day.
God blesses you with a covenant relationship
that is never closed to you or anyone.
We will abide by the word of truth
that survives though heaven and earth pass away.
Amen.   **Amen.**

(See hymns No. 82 and No. 83.)

Pentecost 27
(November 20–26)

Old Testament: Jeremiah 23:1–6
Psalm 93
Epistle: Revelation 1:4b–8
Gospel: John 18:33–37

CALL TO WORSHIP

God reigns; let the earth be glad
God's word is truth; let all people rejoice.
We bow before God's strength and majesty;
we come in awe before God most high.
Grace to you and peace from the One who is
and was and is to come.
God's rule is from everlasting and forevermore;
all creation bows before God's holiness.
Be gathered, then, by God's love and truth,
to worship and make faithful witness.
God is our righteousness and our peace.
We come to be renewed in God's truth.

INVOCATION

Ruler of the universe, Creator of all worlds, Giver of life, we gather as
your own people to praise you and marvel at your goodness to us. Bring
us back from our scattered lives and fragmented loyalties to the shelter of
your fold. Assure us once more of your loving care, and teach us again
that we may bear witness to your truth. Amen.

CALL TO CONFESSION

Come from those scattered places where differences divide and inhumanity dismays. Bring the injustices of a troubled world and the
prejudices and narrowness of your own vision to the only One who can
heal. Let us recognize together that we are sinners in thought and deed,
even as we try to be faithful.

PRAYER OF CONFESSION

Almighty God, whose reign we have denied and whose purposes we have
opposed, we pray for forgiveness and healing. We confess that self-
concern, rather than your will, has motivated us. We have claimed to
follow Jesus, but our discipleship has been halfhearted, and our worship
has been empty of passion and expectation. Turn us around and claim us
for your own purposes. In Jesus' name. Amen.

ASSURANCE OF FORGIVENESS

Christ loves us and frees us from our sins. Those who are of the truth will hear Christ's voice and will bear witness to God's salvation. God is our righteousness and our security; there is no need for us to fear. Amen.

COLLECT

Great Shepherd of Humanity, teach us anew to care for one another, to be just and merciful, to probe the spiritual depths for that connection which is eternal. May the faithful witness of Jesus Christ draw us into communion with you and unite us in your services. Speak now; we are ready to hear. Amen.

OFFERTORY INVITATION

God has multiplied the goodness we enjoy and continues to bless us in every way. How shall we respond to the One who gathers the faithful remnant and entrusts us with the tasks of bringing justice and truth to a troubled world? Let us give account of our stewardship in this time of giving.

OFFERTORY PRAYER

No offering is complete unless we give ourselves with our substance. Take all that is yours and make us partners with Jesus Christ in your ministry of reconciliation. Use us as undershepherds, as instruments of Christ's continuing revelation in the Spirit, as witnesses who live and speak your truth day by day. Amen.

COMMISSION AND BLESSING

Go out to tell the world
that God is alive and in charge.
No evil can have the last word,
for God is greater than any wrong.
God calls us to creative living
and prepares us for our time of dying.
God is the Alpha and Omega,
who is and was and is to come.
Praise be to God who equips us
for the life and ministry we share.
Praise God for truth and righteousness
and for peace that has no end.
Amen.   **Amen.**

(See hymn No. 84.)

Other Special Occasions

Presentation
(February 2)

Old Testament: Malachi 3:1–4
                  Psalm 84 or 24:7–10
Epistle: Hebrews 2:14–18
Gospel: Luke 2:22–40

CALL TO WORSHIP
Blessed are those who come to God's house
singing praises and presenting their best.
We seek the Messenger of God's covenant,
the One who brings God's salvation.
A day in God's courts
is better than ten thousand elsewhere.
We would rather be doorkeepers for God
than dwell in tents of wickedness.
Lift up your heads, O gates and ancient doors,
that the God of hosts may enter in.
God withholds nothing from the upright;
blest are all who trust the God of hosts.

INVOCATION
From the threatening valleys of life where we seek to discern springs of
living water, we come to this oasis where you are known more clearly and
worshiped more devoutly. Together may we discover anew the support of
your covenant love and the strength that comes from times of prayer.
Deliver us from bondage and fear, so our eyes may see your salvation.
Amen.

CALL TO CONFESSION
Come to the Source of Life for renewal, to the refiner's fire for purifica-
tion. God alone can deal with your sin and destroy the power of death.
God is ready to hear all you are ready to confess.

PRAYER OF CONFESSION
O God, our Sun and our Shield, we find ourselves far from you, in
bondage to our worst fears and impulses. We live in the valleys and
shadows rather than in the high hills of aspiration where your light
abounds and sin has no place to hide. Lift us up, O God, lest we sink from
the sight of all that is good and worthy of our attention. Forgive us and
make us whole. In Christ. Amen.

ASSURANCE OF FORGIVENESS
Christ destroys the forces of evil and death and makes expiation for our sin. As Jesus suffered temptation, so now we can face temptation and withstand it in Christ's name. The One who suffered and died for us draws us into living partnership, that forgiveness may be extended to all. Praise God! Amen.

COLLECT
Sometimes you come suddenly, O God, and sometimes a moment at a time. Sometimes we are amazed and awed by evidence of your presence, while at other times we are weighed down by fears that we are alone and abandoned. We lift up our heads and hearts, seeking your consolation and deliverance. Help us now to hear and appropriate the wisdom you would impart. Amen.

OFFERTORY INVITATION
Bring offerings pleasing to God, the first and best of all you have to give. Offer your sacrifices with joy, for God is merciful and faithful. What an opportunity we have to accomplish significant ministries through our tithes and offerings! Let us give with joy!

OFFERTORY PRAYER
O God, if these are not the right offerings that you expect of us, convict us of our poor stewardship and strengthen us to make better choices in the future. Please use what we have given to hasten your rule among us. In Jesus' name. Amen.

COMMISSION AND BLESSING
Blessed are those who have sung praises
and presented their best in God's house.
**We have sought and found salvation
and are eager to share God's goodness.**
Do not go out to dwell in tents of wickedness,
but follow instead paths of righteousness.
**Our hearts and our strength belong to God,
and we wish to keep covenant with our Maker.**
Grow with Christ, in strength and wisdom,
rejoicing in God's blessing and favor.
**May our lives sing for joy to the living God,
who has delivered us from death to life.**
Amen.   **Amen.**

(See hymn No. 85.)

Annunciation
(March 25)

Old Testament: Isaiah 7:10–14
Psalm 40:6–10
Epistle: Hebrews 10:4–10
Gospel: Luke 1:26–38

CALL TO WORSHIP

Greet the congregation of believers
with reminders of God's steadfast love.
God's ears are open to our cries;
God hears us when we call.
Greet one another as brothers and sisters,
persons who find favor with their Creator.
Our ears are open to one another's cries;
we seek to show our care and concern.
This day brings glad news of deliverance,
for God's help is not hidden from us.
We have come to put our trust in God
and to devote ourselves to God's will.

INVOCATION

We have come once more that you may write your law within us and
create new depths of community among us. Make your presence and
your purposes clear to us; then grant us the courage to live by your design
rather than our own. Amen.

CALL TO CONFESSION

Surely we weary God with our arrogance and our misuse of the gifts God
has granted us. But God does not grow weary of sincere penitence and
genuine recommitment. Let us seek to understand and confess our sin
that God may forgive.

PRAYER OF CONFESSION

Great God, whose attention and favor we cannot win by mighty efforts,
we confess our preoccupation with our own narrow concerns. Some of us
have such low opinions of ourselves that we cannot believe you care about
us. Some of us loom so large over our own horizons that all else is blocked
from our view. At either extreme, and many places in between, we lose
sight of your creative love and judgment that calls us into partnership
with your eternal purposes. Forgive our sin and help us to know the joy of
full participation in your way. Amen.

ASSURANCE OF FORGIVENESS

With God, nothing is impossible. The worst you have done, and the good you have avoided are swept up in God's forgiving love as you are truly penitent and ready to give yourselves fully to God's purposes. Walk today in newness of life. Amen.

COLLECT

Send your Holy Spirit to break through our self-satisfied, self-limited existence, that we may experience the depths of your saving love and the awe and wonder of your favor. Establish within us your new order by which we are united with you and one another as you reign among us. Amen.

OFFERTORY INVITATION

God does not require ritual offerings. This time of giving is not to satisfy God's claims on us, or to win God's attention. Rather, we give out of gratitude for Christ's selfless sacrifice and God's continuing generosity—and because we care about our sisters and brothers.

OFFERTORY PRAYER

Thank you, God, for your faithfulness and steadfast love by which we have been blessed and enabled to share. We delight to do your will and to share in the ministry and mission of the church. Bless and multiply all our efforts, we pray. Amen.

COMMISSION AND BLESSING

Greet a world of unbelievers
with demonstrations of God's steadfast love.
**In word and deed we would respond
to all whose burdens we can help to carry.**
Greet a world of sisters and brothers
who doubt that you or God really care.
**We seek to be truthful in our outreach
and sincere in our service.**
Greet the opportunities of today,
for God goes with you.
**We go forth to do your will, O God,
for with you nothing is impossible!**
Amen.   **Amen.**

(See hymn No. 86.)

Visitation
(May 31)

Old Testament: 1 Samuel 2:1–10
Psalm 113
Epistle: Romans 12:9–16b
Gospel: Luke 1:39–57

CALL TO WORSHIP

Come, all who feel barren and broken.
Come, lowly of the earth, to God's exultation.
God raises the poor from the dust
and lifts up the needy from the ash heaps of life.
Come, all who are hungry and thirsty.
Come, all who are proud and arrogant.
The full have hired themselves out for bread,
while the hungry have been satisfied.
In love and judgment among all people,
God turns our expectations upside down.
Praise God from sunrise to sunset;
blessed be the name of our Sovereign, forever.

INVOCATION

God of All Knowledge, by whom all our actions are weighed, grant us sincerity of purpose and openness to your movement among us as we gather for worship. Lift up the lowly, and humble the arrogant among us, that we may meet on common ground before your majesty and glory. May all we think and do in this hour be worthy of your name. Amen.

CALL TO CONFESSION

Our judgment of people and events may not match God's assessment. The way we live our lives may not coincide with our profession of faith. We come to this time of confession to attune ourselves once more to God's purposes and to seek the strength we need to be faithful.

PRAYER OF CONFESSION

Mighty One, we have been haughty and proud, congratulating ourselves for who we are. We have been lowly and broken, blaming you for what we are not. The circles of our concern have been narrow. Our relationship with you has been one-sided. Forgive us, God, for we want to change, to be in tune with your love, that we may care about ourselves and others in new ways. Hear us and help us. In Christ's name. Amen.

ASSURANCE OF FORGIVENESS

God judges the ends of the earth with holiness and compassion. The Mighty One does good things for all who are open to the rule of self-giving love in their lives. God's mercy is from generation to generation; it is real to all who repent and believe today. Receive God's gift. Amen.

COLLECT

Sovereign God, remove arrogance from our mouths and unstop our ears, that we may hear your word aright and be strengthened by it to do your will. May we learn to praise you in all circumstances and to be affectionately devoted to one another. Keep us from being dominated by all that divides us, that we may find new grounds for unity with all your children. Amen.

OFFERTORY INVITATION

Contribute to the needs of the saints—to those who lead our church, to those who minister on our behalf around the world, to all who need God's word and any other necessities of life. May our offerings be a faithful response to God's love.

OFFERTORY PRAYER

For all the good things you have done for us we give thanks, O God. Use these offerings to fill the hungry with good things, to bring harmony among your children, to increase among us the knowledge and practice of your love. To these ends we dedicate ourselves with our gifts. Amen.

COMMISSION AND BLESSING

Go forth as God's people, forgiven and healed.
Go forth, lifted up and empowered.
   We have been cared for and fed,
   protected, enriched, and strengthened.
Let love be genuine among you;
hate evil and hold fast to all that is good.
   We will devote ourselves to one another,
   rejoicing and weeping together.
Never flag in zeal; be aglow with the Spirit;
serve God in all you say and do.
   Blessed be the name of our God forever,
   from the rising of the sun to its setting.
Amen.   **Amen.**

(See hymn No. 87.)

Holy Cross
(September 14)

Old Testament: Numbers 21:4b–9
Psalm 98:1–5
Epistle: 1 Corinthians 1:18–24
Gospel: John 3:13–17

CALL TO WORSHIP

Come away from your impatience and despair,
from a wisdom that neither sees nor understands.
Why should we flatter God with our tongues
when our hearts sense no vision or hope?
Give ear to God's teaching; listen and hear.
God has not destroyed you in wrath and anger.
Dare we believe that Christ came, not to condemn,
but to be the instrument of our salvation?
Sing a new song to God, who has done marvelous things;
remember God's steadfast love and faithfulness.
Make a joyful noise to God, all the earth.
Praise God with joyous songs; sing praises!

INVOCATION

While you are never far away, God of All Times and Places, we wander far in our thoughts and actions. We forget your loving care and provision, and often feel abandoned. So we invoke your presence, not to gain your attention, but that you may awaken our awareness. Help us to see and taste the food and water you provide for our spirits. In Jesus' name. Amen.

CALL TO CONFESSION

Seek God earnestly. Remember and repent. The cross, which is folly to the perishing, is the power of God to those who are being saved. Let us come to God, our Rock and our Redeemer, in prayer that is sincere and from our hearts.

PRAYER OF CONFESSION

We have sinned, for we have spoken against you, O God, and against your messengers. We do not understand the cross or the One who was crucified. Why would another die for us? How can Christ's death save us? Yet, even as we pray, we are compelled by wisdom and power beyond our grasp, by a love that will not let us go. Forgive us, God, and lift us up to share in the life you intend for us. Amen.

ASSURANCE OF FORGIVENESS

God is compassionate and forgiving, making foolish the wisdom of the world and restoring us to covenant. Whoever believes shall not perish, but have eternal life. God loves us. Enjoy and celebrate that love. Bask in it and pass it on. Praise God with instruments and voices. Let everything and everyone praise God! Amen.

COLLECT

Holy God, without whom we would die in the wilderness of our sin, we come to your steadfast love and faithfulness, eager to be reassured and inspired. Help us to embrace the cross of Christ as an ongoing reality among us, that we may sense eternity in the midst of time and realize your saving love in all our relationships. Amen.

OFFERTORY INVITATION

It is the foolishness of God to give to us over and over, without counting the cost. How shall we respond? Our offerings are a beginning.

OFFERTORY PRAYER

For the food you give us, even when we call it worthless, for water that refreshes and cleanses, for the gift of your Only Child to express the power of your love and forgiveness, we give thanks, Gracious God. Bless and multiply our efforts to make fitting response. In Jesus' name. Amen.

COMMISSION AND BLESSING

Carry forward the cross of your redemption;
it is the power of God for the world's salvation.
We would offer God's forgiving love
to a world desperate for good news.
God saves through the folly of what you preach,
by word and living example.
We dare to proclaim Christ crucified,
the wisdom and power of Almighty God.
The words of God's mouth are in your ears;
the power of God's love is in your hearts.
Believers shall not perish, but have eternal life;
make a joyful noise to God, all the earth!
Amen.   **Amen.**

(See hymn No. 88.)

All Saints
(November 1, or First Sunday in November)

Old Testament: Revelation 21:1–6a
　　　　　　　Psalm 24:1–6
Epistle: Colossians 1:9–14
Gospel: John 11:32–44

CALL TO WORSHIP

Come, saints of God, to a new heaven and earth,
to the holy city, God's new Jerusalem.
The dwelling place of God is with humanity;
God wipes away the tears from our eyes.
The earth is God's and the fullness thereof,
the world and all who dwell therein.
Who shall ascend to the hill of God,
and who shall stand in God's holy place?
All whose hands are clean and hearts pure
shall know God's vindication and blessing.
We give thanks to God, who has qualified us
to share the inheritance of the saints.

INVOCATION

Great God, who makes all things new, create new attitudes and awareness
within us as we join the saints of all times and places in singing your
praises. Fill us with the knowledge of your will. Lift us up and unbind us
in this time of worship so we may serve, to your honor and glory. Through
Christ. Amen.

CALL TO CONFESSION

When we are called saints the idea jars us, for we are not saintly people.
But we are seekers after God's will, who have been powerfully claimed by
Jesus Christ. Remembering who we are intended to be, let us come to
God's holy place to find forgiveness, healing, and empowerment.

PRAYER OF CONFESSION

O God, our God, we confess that we have lifted up our souls to what is
false. We have deceived ourselves and other people. The life we have led
is not worthy of our Sovereign, Jesus Christ. Our words and actions have
imprisoned others rather than setting them free, and we ourselves are
bound by our prejudices and inhumanity. Forgive us, O God, for we
cannot live in our deceit and unfaithfulness. Amen.

ASSURANCE OF FORGIVENESS

God delivers us from the dominion of evil. Come out of the graves of your sinful living. There is redemption and forgiveness of sin in Jesus Christ. Be strengthened by the power of God's glorious might to lead a new life and bear much fruit. Amen.

COLLECT

Move us beyond your healing and forgiveness to take further steps of faithfulness, O God, our Alpha and Omega. As the former things pass away, grant us clearer vision of the new realities you place before us. Purify our hearts, fill us with the knowledge of your will, and help us to see and proclaim your glory. Amen.

OFFERTORY INVITATION

Come to this time of giving, not with regrets, but bearing good fruit, not out of compulsion, but realizing the joy of passing on what you have received. How wonderful it is that the inheritance of the saints is ours to share!

OFFERTORY PRAYER

We pour out our offerings, O God, that others may believe. We trust you to bring your new day to all our sisters and brothers. May we manage all your gifts according to your purposes, in Christ. Amen.

COMMISSION AND BLESSING

The dwelling place of God is with people;
let others know that God is with them.
God is in our crying and our pain,
wiping away the tears that blind us.
Be strengthened by all the power of God's might,
for endurance and patience, with joy.
God is in our fears and our many deaths,
untying the knots that bind us.
Embrace God's new heaven and earth,
and see the world's people with new eyes.
Behold, God makes all things new;
we will be God's own people, forever and ever.
Amen. **Amen.**

(See hymn No. 89.)

Thanksgiving Day

Old Testament: Joel 2:21–27
Psalm 126
Epistle: 1 Timothy 2:1–7
Gospel: Matthew 6:25–33

CALL TO WORSHIP

Come, all who are anxious or ashamed.
Come, all who are sad and grieving.
**We rejoice in the abundant gifts of God
and give thanks for our salvation.**
God has blessed us with a rich harvest
from tree, vine, and field.
**We rejoice in the abundant gifts of God
and give thanks for our salvation.**
We have been clothed and fed,
and blessed with an outpouring of God's truth.
**We rejoice in the abundant gifts of God
and give thanks for our salvation.**

INVOCATION

God of the Harvest, we bring our gratitude and praise for rich soil, abundant rainfall, and life-giving energy from the sun. For the plenty that surrounds us, we give thanks. Remembering all who have toiled to produce our food and transport it, we rejoice. May these moments of thanksgiving spill over in generous spirits and unselfish acts of sharing. Amen.

CALL TO CONFESSION

Jesus said, Do not be anxious about what you will eat or drink or wear, for life is more than food and the body more than clothing. Let us come confessing our preoccupation with things and our needless anxiety.

PRAYER OF CONFESSION

O God, we have worried about possessions and lost sleep over matters beyond our control. We have forgotten you as the source of all good things and the resource to strengthen us when our energy is drained and our hope exhausted. We have misused your gifts and invested our time in pursuits that tear down and destroy rather than create and build. Forgive us, God, and set us on a new and right path. We pray in Jesus' name. Amen.

ASSURANCE OF FORGIVENESS
God desires all people to be saved, to come to a knowledge of truth. Jesus Christ is our mediator before the Eternal and our link with all that is beyond our knowing. Praise God for our salvation in Christ. Amen.

COLLECT
Your blessings, O God, overflow in joy and laughter among us. Use these moments, when we are alerted to all your gifts, to teach your truth and increase our faith. Lessen needless anxiety within and among us, we pray, and free us to seek your realm before all else. Amen.

OFFERTORY INVITATION
Lilies of the field do not spin, and birds of the air do not gather into barns. We cannot hoard the abundance of God for our own use. Let us share it!

OFFERTORY PRAYER
We give because we are grateful. We give to praise you, O God, and rejoice in blessings beyond our awareness or deserving. We share because that seems our joyous duty amid the unequal distribution of your abundance. Increase our joy and our generosity. For Jesus' sake. Amen.

COMMISSION AND BLESSING
God frees us from anxiety, guilt, and shame
to go forth as servants of the Most High.
We will serve with joy
wherever God sends us.
Seek first the realm of God
and all other things shall be yours as well.
We will lift up our prayers,
that all people might know God's truth.
Witness to your faith before others,
for God has appointed you to speak.
We know God values us
and will supply the help we need.
Amen.   **Amen.**

(See hymn No. 90.)

Appendix of Related Hymns

At least one new hymn text, based on the day's scripture readings, is provided for each occasion in the church year. These are supplemented by a few additional songs created for special occasions, such as farewells, clergy recognitions, anniversaries, weddings, and funerals. In all, one hundred new hymns are included.

The meter for each hymn is noted at its upper right-hand corner, indicating the number of syllables in each line of the poem. Traditional church music has been structured to match this format. Consult the metrical index of a standard hymnal to find tunes written to accommodate the number of lines and syllables in the text.

For your convenience, a specific tune is suggested for each hymn. Names applied to popular hymn tunes are fairly standard. Thus you can consult an alphabetical index of tunes as another way to locate the music I had in mind as I wrote the words. Usually there are several other tunes that would fit the text just as well.

You may print the words of hymns in your worship order, noting their source as authorized on the copyright page at the front of this book.

In the topical index of hymns, beginning on page 239, you have a tool for locating additional hymns in this book that might fit your worship theme.

Hymns for the Advent Season

1. Creator, Be Not Angry

First Sunday of Advent—B

7.6.7.6.D.
(AURELIA)

LAVON BAYLER

Creator, be not angry
At our unfaithfulness,
For wrong has lured us elsewhere
Than your intent to bless.
Our hearts are hard within us
While enemies enjoy
The specter of our failure
And watch our sins destroy.

Before you nations tremble,
And we are filled with fear,
For in our long denial
We have not felt you near.
Your goodness we've forgotten
And oft' denied your name.
O Gentle Shepherd, hear us,
As we our faith reclaim.

O, lead us and restore us
By saving love and grace.
We bow, as clay, before you,
The Potter, whose embrace
Calls forth the best within us
And shapes and molds with care,
That we may trust your mercy
And loyalty declare.

The Sovereign Christ, whose coming
This season, we expect,
Brings promise of forgiveness
And healthy self-respect.
With Spirit's gifts abounding,
Our goals we readjust,
To watch and wait, with courage,
And venture forth in trust. Amen.

2. God Offers Forgiveness

Second Sunday of Advent—B

LAVON BAYLER

11.11.11.11.
(MULLER)

God offers forgiveness and comfort to all
Who, from their despair, shall upon God's name call.
The glory of God shall this day be revealed
As God gently leads and our warfare is healed.

Believers experience God's peace deep within
And know steadfast love as they turn from their sin.
In faithfulness, come, that the Sovereign may save
And earth yield the increase a righteous God gave.

God's messenger calls us and bids us prepare
The way for our Savior to show God's great care.
To untie Christ's sandals is more than we rate,
For Christ, who is coming, is worthy and great.

God's new day is dawning in heaven and earth.
A voice in the wilderness summons to birth
A godliness built on repentance and trust
And righteousness working for causes more just. Amen.

3. Rejoice, God's Spirit Comes

Third Sunday of Advent—B

LAVON BAYLER

8.6.8.6. (C.M.)
(BEATITUDO)

Rejoice, God's Spirit comes to us,
Empow'ring us to share
Good tidings with all suffering ones
And freedom everywhere.

Stand with the brokenhearted folk
Whenever they are hurt;
Release from prison those oppressed,
God's justice to assert.

The proud are scattered and put down,
The mighty rich dismayed,
For God has chosen humble ones
Who follow, unafraid.

Those souls who magnify the Lord,
Who pray, give thanks, and praise,
Shall know the power of God within
And mercy through their days.

We seek to know the peace of God,
Whose faithfulness makes whole,
Who pardons us and sanctifies
In body, mind, and soul.

Rejoice that Christ has brought God's light
To show us better ways,
That we may follow where Christ leads
And glad thanksgiving raise. Amen.

---

4. All Things Are Possible

Fourth Sunday of Advent—B

8.8.8.8. *(L.M.)*
LAVOR BAYLER   (ERFURT)

All things are possible with God
Who knows the wayward paths we've trod,
Who favors us with love and care,
Whose faithfulness is everywhere.

God's covenant has drawn us in
To steadfast love and discipline.
God offers vision and a name
To those who Jesus Christ proclaim.

We find new strength to help each day
As God gives rest along life's way.
We face the future unafraid,
For God will reign, as Jesus prayed.

Obedient, affirmative,
By Jesus' teaching, we will live,
Each day's new mystery explore,
To God be glory evermore. Amen.

Hymns for the Christmas Season

5. We Hear Your New Song

Christmas Eve/Day—A,B,C

LAVON BAYLER

8.7.8.7.D.
(CONSTANCE)

We hear your new song on the earth,
Great God of our salvation.
A blessed hope is brought to birth,
Resounding through creation.
As heav'nly choirs proclaim your worth,
Announcing incarnation,
Will we respond with joy and mirth,
And sing in glad elation?

Or is no room for Bethle'm's child
Found in each place we tarry?
Will God's Messiah be reviled
While other folks make merry?
And will we live unreconciled
'Though 'round our necks we carry
The cross we've made a symbol mild,
Its full demands to bury?

O come, as mighty Prince of Peace,
As Couns'lor ever with us,
That we, from gloom, may find release
And truly follow Jesus.
Let worldly passions now decrease
That Truth within may seize us,
And cause all war and strife to cease,
As Christ redeems and frees us. Amen.

6. By a Manger Far Away

Christmas Eve/Day—A,B,C

7.7.7.7.7.7.
(DIX)

LAVON BAYLER

By a manger far away
Shepherds knelt, in awe, to pray.
Summoned by angelic choirs,
Leaving flocks and warming fires,
They made haste to Bethlehem,
Sharing what had come to them.

"Glory be to God on high;
Do not be afraid to die.
Neither be afraid to live
And, for Christ, your all to give.
Tell what you have seen and heard;
Share, with all, God's living word."

When the grace of God appears,
We are rescued from our fears.
No more can oppressor's rod
Keep us from the will of God.
Justice comes, with peace to reign,
And true equity sustain.

May we serve, and heed God's call
Which, in Christ, now comes to all,
And declare the wondrous joy
Earthly pow'rs cannot destroy,
Lifted up to prayer and praise,
Follow Christ through all our days. Amen.

7. God Reigns, Let Earth Rejoice!

Christmas Day (Alternate 1)—A, B, C

6.6.8.6. (S.M.)
(ST. THOMAS)

LAVON BAYLER

God reigns, let earth rejoice!
Salvation comes today.

Hear angels sing the great good news
That love is here to stay.

God seeks each wand'ring one
And offers us new light
In which to see the Word-made-flesh
Beyond the manger bright.

God reassures, empow'rs,
The witness we would make.
As simple shepherds shared good news,
Our tasks we undertake.

God sends us forth to serve
As builders on life's way.
Redeemed of God, we testify
Through actions ev'ry day. Amen.

---

8. Break Forth in Singing

Christmas Day (Alternate 2)—A, B, C

LAVON BAYLER

IRREGULAR METER
(CRUSADERS' HYMN)

Break forth in singing;
Raise songs of joyous praise.
God's Word has come in the Human One,
Born in a manger,
Heralded by angels,
This child and heir, God's victory won.

God reigns among us
Now in the Word-made-flesh.
Let lyre and trumpet and roaring sea
Publish the news of peace,
Our caring to increase,
Until all humankind is free.

Comfort God's people;
Win their salvation.
This is the mandate of Jesus' birth.
Hear what the prophets say,
Glory in Jesus' way.
'Til Christ is known through all the earth. Amen.

9. Give Thanks to God

Christmas 1—B
(Based on Psalm 111)

10.10.10.10.10.10.
(YORKSHIRE)

LAVON BAYLER

Give thanks to God with all your heart and soul.
Great are the works of God which we extol.
Gracious and merciful, our God supplies
Food that we need to live, and hears our cries.
Wisdom and faith, God promises to grant
To all who enter into covenant.

Honor and majesty are in God's deeds.
Moment by moment God allays our needs.
Faithful and just, God's righteousness endures;
And through our lives God comes and reassures.
We will not fear the God whom we adore,
But live in awe and trust forevermore. Amen.

10. Rejoice, the Time Has Come

Christmas 1—B

8.6.8.6.7.6.8.6.
(ST. LOUIS)

LAVON BAYLER

Rejoice, the time has fully come,
And God has sent a child
To be the carrier of good news
That we are reconciled.
As heirs, released from bondage,
We, too, can claim a place
Amid God's children who aspire
To see God face to face.

In worship, fasting Anna prayed,
"Thanks be to God above!
This child is surely meant to be
Proclaimer of God's love."
Then Simeòn, too, gave blessing
As he felt God had willed.

"In peace, now let your servant die;
My dream has been fulfilled."

As Jesus grew in Nazareth,
So we are called to grow
In strength and wisdom God supplies
To those who care to know.
The way of truth and service
Shall be our constant aim.
God clothes us with salvation's power
And calls us by Christ's name.

We cannot long our silence keep
As we receive God's gift.
We will not rest while others bear
Oppression we can lift.
The peace of God compels us
To share that peace with all
Our sisters and our brothers, who
Must also hear God's call. Amen.

---

11. God, Who Made This Earth

January 1 (New Year)—B

8.7.8.7.8.7.
(REGENT SQUARE)

LAVON BAYLER

God, who made this earth of beauty,
Grant us now a fresh new year,
Calling forth to joyful duty
Those whose worship is sincere.
In this season of beginnings,
May your will for us be clear.

Reigning God, beyond our knowing,
Glorious is your name on earth.
All your mercy overflowing
Summons us to claim our worth.
In this season of beginnings,
May our spirits know rebirth.

Food and drink and toil, you've granted
To enhance humanity.
In our hearts and minds, you've planted
Visions of eternity.

In this season of beginnings
Show us our identity.

You have offered times for speaking
And some moments to be still.
While our lives are filled with seeking,
Loss may also show your will.
In this season of beginnings,
Come, your purpose to fulfill. Amen.

---

12. God of All People

January 1—Celebration of Jesus and Mary—A, B, C

11.10.11.10.

LAVON BAYLER

(MORNING STAR)

God of all people, whose glory is chanted
Through all the nations who honor your name,
Hear now our thanks for the gift you have granted
In Jesus Christ, whose good news we proclaim.

We would rejoice with the shepherds whose praises
Heralded a day of salvation brought near,
Joining in thanks for your pow'r which amazes
Nations and people you rescue from fear.

We seek your will in our smallest endeavor,
That Jesus' name may be honored on earth.
May our Creator's good purpose and pleasure
Lift our commitment to glorious rebirth.

Bless us and keep us as now, in your presence,
We are forgiv'n and experience release.
May we not stray into feelings of absence
But live each day in your love and your peace. Amen.

---

13. God, Whose Word Brought Light

Christmas 2—A, B, C

7.7.7.7.D. with refrain

LAVON BAYLER

(MENDELSSOHN)

God, whose Word has brought us light,
Grant us power to live aright.

May we always sing your praise,
Everywhere, through all our days.
Joy emerges from our tears
As you comfort through the years,
Leading with a shepherd's care
To new life beyond compare.
We, your children, rise to bring
All the thanks our hearts would sing.

In your goodness we abide,
Using gifts that you provide:
Flowing waters, finest wheat,
Gardens full of things to eat,
Grace that meets our earnest plea
That forgiveness we may see,
Truth that turns us from despair
To the hope we now declare.
We, your children, rise to bring
All the thanks our hearts would sing.

Shine upon our lives today,
That Christ's path may be our way.
Gather all who seek your face,
Saints and sinners, claiming grace.
Bring from places far and near
Blind and lame and all who fear,
That your wisdom may be known
And your glory clearly shown.
We, your children, rise to bring
All the thanks our hearts would sing.

Word made flesh before our eyes,
Christ of God, we recognize;
Come that we may all receive
Trusting power to believe.
Grant us holiness, we pray;
Dwell among us day by day.
In your Spirit may we live,
Blessing you for all you give.
We, your children, rise to bring
All the thanks our hearts would sing. Amen.

Hymns for the Epiphany Season

14. Rise and Shine Today

Epiphany—A,B,C

10.8.10.8.8.8.
(MARGARET)

LAVON BAYLER

Rise and shine today, for your light has come,
And the shadows of earth shall flee,
And the glory of God will be seen by all
Who will lift up their eyes to see.
Rejoice, for a star is leading
All who reach t'ward God's mystery.

Nations seek the light, as they bring their gifts,
To acclaim Jesus' sov'reignty.
From the east and west, and the north and south,
People come, just to bend the knee.
Rejoice, for a star is leading
All who reach t'ward God's mystery.

God will judge the poor with a righteous hand
That, with justice, shall set them free
From oppression's grip and from violence,
And affirm their humanity.
Rejoice, for a star is leading
All who reach t'ward God's mystery.

We are heirs of grace and God's promises
That will shape us eternally,
For the least of us is made rich in Christ,
With a radiant humility.
Rejoice, for a star is leading
All who reach t'ward God's mystery. Amen.

15. Glory to God

First Sunday After Epiphany—B
(Baptism of Our Sovereign)

8.6.8.6. (*C.M.*)

LAVON BAYLER

(ST. AGNES)

Glory to God, who blesses us
With inner peace and light.
In flashing flame and flowing stream,
God comes with pow'r and might.

Before God's majesty and grace,
We bow our knees to pray,
Seeking forgiveness from our sin,
And help along life's way.

Come, Holy Spirit, to baptize
With cleansing waters pure,
With sweeping fires that burn within,
With courage to endure.

In Jesus, your beloved Child,
Your purposes are shown.
We turn to Christ with faith and hope
To know as we are known. Amen.

16. Speak, O Sovereign God

Second Sunday After Epiphany—B

8.7.8.7.D.

LAVON BAYLER

(NETTLETON)

Speak, O Sovereign God most holy,
For your servants hear your voice,
Giving selves to serve you solely,
That your people may rejoice.
Let us hear your clear direction,
Calling each of us by name.
May we bring devout reflection
To the faith our lips proclaim.

Souls are thirsty in their seeking
For our God who sanctifies.
Hear our silence and our seeking,
God of love, beyond the skies.
Come each day to reign among us,
And to lift our thoughts above;
May we know your power within us,
As we give ourselves in love.

Temples of the Holy Spirit,
We our God would glorify
In our bodies and each unit
Of the church which reaches high.
Lamb of God, we've come to see you
As the Christ God sent to save.
We would follow, as did Andrew,
Faithful, though we risk the grave. Amen.

17. Follow Where Jesus Leads

Third Sunday After Epiphany—B

6.6.8.6.D. (S.M.D.)
(DIADEMATA)

LAVON BAYLER

Follow where Jesus leads,
For time is growing short;
The Savior meets our human needs
And tells of God's support.
God's realm is now at hand;
Repent, turn, and believe.
The steadfast love in which we stand,
May all in need receive.

God is our refuge strong,
In whom we find our worth.
All hearts to Jesus Christ belong
Who follow here on earth.
Self-centered pride is lost
In God's equality.
We long to serve, whate'er the cost,
Without anxiety.

The Holy Spirit's power
Calls us to leave the past,
To recognize within this hour
The only truths that last.
No riches, fame, or might
Will finally win the day.
We trust our God to give us sight
As old worlds pass away. Amen.

---

18. We Give You Thanks

Fourth Sunday After Epiphany—B

7.6.7.6.D.
(LANCASHIRE)

LAVON BAYLER

We give you thanks, our Parent,
For all your wondrous deeds;
Your graciousness and mercy
Provide for all our needs.
In covenant we worship
And hail your majesty,
Proclaiming to all nations
Your love, that sets us free.

Your works are great among us,
Your righteousness endures;
Your faithfulness and justice
Our heritage assures.
Now, in this congregation,
We honor all you've done
And, trusting you forever,
Share love with everyone.

We celebrate your prophets.
The clear word we would heed,
That, knowing your intention,
Our own and others' need,
We might reach out in service
That leads no one astray
But lifts us all, believing,
Into your fresh new day.

O Sovereign God of Ages,
Whose word is like a fire,
Burn now within each conscience,
Our actions to inspire.
Make each a faithful servant,
Obeying your commands,
That witness which we offer
May help another stand. Amen.

---

19. Praise Our God

Fifth Sunday After Epiphany—B

8.7.8.7.D.
(ST. ASAPH)

LAVON BAYLER

Praise our God with great thanksgiving
For the healing hands of love,
Binding up our wounded spirits
With a power from above.
Understanding all our problems,
All the sins we would avert.
God is gracious to forgive us,
Lifting up the ones who hurt.

Through our days of empty living,
Through our nights of deep distress,
God will not forsake or leave us,
Even in our bitterness.
Rains supply our need for water,
By God's hand we all are fed.
We will rise from evil's bondage,
By God's mercy comforted.

Rise in hope, God's sons and daughters,
By God's steadfast love and grace.
Greet the day with prayer and praising,
All its moments to embrace.
We must preach the gospel story,
Share God's blessing with the world,
Loving, caring, healing, praying
That Christ's truth may be unfurled. Amen.

20. O God, We Seek You

Sixth Sunday After Epiphany—B

8.8.8.8. *(L.M.)*

LAVON BAYLER

(BROOKFIELD)

O God, we seek you in distress
That we may greet, with eagerness,
The race of life you set before
Your people, now and evermore.

May we, as children of your grace,
Look deep within ourselves to face
All selfish thoughts and hidden deeds
That turn us from another's needs.

Your steadfast love and healing pow'r,
Give to each worshiper this hour.
May all who trust you turn from sin
To find new health and strength within.

Instruct and counsel us today,
Lest we rebel and turn away
From life that follows your intent;
Grant faith to go where we are sent. Amen.

21. Blessed Are God's People

Seventh Sunday After Epiphany—B

10.10.10.10.10.

LAVON BAYLER

(OLD 124TH)

Blessed are God's people, who confess their sin,
Seeking forgiveness for the wrong within,
Working to change their evil thoughts and deeds,
As they acknowledge all their deepest needs.
Blessed are God's people, who confess their sin.

Blessed are God's people, who respond with praise,
Walking with Jesus through their length of days,
Led by the Spirit, lifted up by grace,

Finding God's newest gifts in every place.
Blessed are God's people, who respond with praise.

Blessed are God's people, who protect the poor,
Lending a hand as suff'ring ones endure,
Helping the brokenhearted find relief,
With loving presence in their time of grief.
Blessed are God's people, who protect the poor. Amen.

---

22. Hear the Voice of God

Eighth Sunday After Epiphany—B

8.7.8.7.D.
(VESPER HYMN)

LAVON BAYLER

Hear the voice of God, so tender,
Gath'ring us, in righteousness,
Giving, as our sure defender,
Steadfast love and faithfulness.
Bless God's holy name together,
As the Spirit brings new life.
Giving, as our sure defender,
Steadfast love and faithfulness.

God is healing and forgiving
Creatures who are sore distressed,
Op'ning doors to hopeful living,
As, by love, we're daily blessed.
Bless God's holy name together,
As the Spirit brings new life.
Op'ning doors to hopeful living,
As, by love, we're daily blessed.

List'ning to the Spirit's guiding,
Rather than the written code,
We, in covenant abiding,
Seek to write our letters bold.
Bless God's holy name together
As the Spirit brings new life.
We, in covenant abiding,
Seek to write our letters bold.

Shed the old wineskins of warfare
For the fresh new wines of peace,
Knowing God sustains our welfare
With a love that will not cease.
Bless God's holy name together
As the Spirit brings new life.
Knowing God sustains our welfare,
With a love that will not cease. Amen.

---

23. Speak, Mighty One

Last Sunday After Epiphany—B
(Transfiguration)

8.6.8.6.D. *(C.M.D.)*
LAVON BAYLER
(ELLACOMBE)

Speak, Mighty One, who summons earth
From dawn to end of day,
Who judges people's faithfulness
By your own righteous way.
Before you comes devouring fire,
Around you tempests roar.
The glist'ning clouds may hide your face,
While whirlwinds speak your pow'r.

Let light shine out of darkness drear,
Great God of heav'n and earth,
That we may see your Word revealed,
And celebrate Christ's worth.
As, high upon the mountaintop,
Disciples heard your voice,
We, too, would listen for your truth
And in your work rejoice.

Empow'r each person gathered with
Your Spirit's double share.
That those who follow Christ may now
Elijah's mantle wear.
As servants for the sake of Christ,
Our lives would show your care,
And to your covenant be true
Both here and everywhere. Amen.

Hymns for Lent

24. Have Mercy, God

Ash Wednesday—A, B, C

8.8.8.8. *(L.M.)*

LAVON BAYLER (TALLIS' CANON)

Have mercy, God, according to
Your steadfast love, which sees us through.
Wash our iniquity away
And cleanse us from all sin today.

Against you only have we sinned,
Rejecting your inviting wind,
The Spirit, who would make things right
Within our hearts and in your sight.

Teach us your wisdom, day by day,
That we may journey in your way,
As Christ's redeeming love destroys
The falsehood that defeats our joys.

As your salvation sets us free,
Forgiving, with this guarantee,
That evil will be washed away,
We claim your promised fresh new day. Amen.

25. Blow Trumpets in Zion

Ash Wednesday—A, B, C

11.11.11.11.

LAVON BAYLER (ST. DENIO)

Blow trumpets in Zion, for God has drawn near,
Recalling a people to fast and to hear
The cries of deep grieving and searching of hearts,
That lead to salvation Christ Jesus imparts.

Behold, the acceptable time is today
For seeking forgiveness, adopting Christ's way.

For welcoming grace, and God's righteous decrees,
By giving ourselves, our Creator to please.

Let praying and giving be done quietly,
That others scarce notice your deep piety.
In secret, turn now, with your gifts and your prayers,
To God, who rewards, and assuages our cares. Amen.

---

26. God's Rainbow Covenant

First Sunday of Lent—B

6.6.8.6.D. (S.M.D.)

LAVON BAYLER

(TERRA BEATA)

God's rainbow covenant
Is shared with humankind
That we may know God's promises
In heart and soul and mind.
God's rainbow covenant
Assures us we can trust
In God's salvation, freely given,
With mercy, kind and just.

God's rainbow covenant
Now calls us to repent
That we may not be put to shame
When truly penitent.
God's rainbow covenant,
Says God, in steadfast love,
Remembers not our former sins,
But points our thoughts above.

God's rainbow covenant
Is meant to teach God's way
Of faithfulness and loving care
As God transforms each day.
God's rainbow covenant
Includes Christ's sacrifice,
That we may claim new life today:
God's offer, without price. Amen.

27. God, Who Offers Life

First Sunday of Lent—B
(A Baptismal Hymn)

8.5.8.5.
(BULLINGER)

LAVON BAYLER

God, who offers life fulfilling,
Hear our praise today,
As we bring to you our children;
Baptize them, we pray.

We believe your precious promise,
Off'ring life anew,
As your cleansing waters free us
To be good and true.

Thank you, God, for all our loved ones,
Children of your care.
We embrace your Living Spirit,
And our vows declare. Amen.

28. The Works of God

Second Sunday of Lent—B

8.6.8.6. (C.M.)
(MEDITATION)

LAVON BAYLER

The works of God are wonderful,
Surpassing all our dreams.
God's miracles and judgments come
To interrupt our schemes.

In covenant God promises
New life, by faith and grace.
For Christ has died, and lives again,
Trespasses to erase.

All those who want to follow Christ
Must selfishness deny,
And, taking risks of faithfulness,
On God alone rely. Amen.

29. Let All Our Words

Third Sunday of Lent—B

8.8.8.8. (L.M.)
(MARYTON)

LAVON BAYLER

Let all our words and thoughts be pure,
And all our actions strong and sure,
Rooted in faithfulness to thee,
Great God, beyond all history.

By your command, we seek to live,
To you our loyalty we give.
No other gods will we pursue,
No graven images construe.

We will not take your name in vain
Or holy Sabbath times profane.
Parents we'll honor, day by day,
In keeping with your holy way.

You have commanded, "Do not kill."
Adult'ry is against your will.
False witness, stealing, coveting
All violate the love you bring.

O, clear us, God, from secret sin
And purify our lives within,
That word and deed may coincide,
And Christ, within each one, abide. Amen.

30. How Shall We Sing?

Fourth Sunday of Lent—B

8.6.8.6. (C.M.)
(MARTYRDOM)

LAVON BAYLER

How shall we sing when we are sad?
When life is filled with pain?
When we are haunted by our sins,
And goodness seems in vain?

In exile from our own best selves,
And from our friends as well,
We long your promises to claim,
Your great good news to tell.

But love is hidden from our sight
And mercy seems unreal.
Our works have never been enough,
Life's goodness to reveal.

O, lead from shadows into light,
From sin into your grace,
And bring us to eternal life
Within your love's embrace. Amen.

---

31. Within Your Temple

Fifth Sunday of Lent—B

8.8.8.8. (*L.M.*)
(HAMBURG)

LAVON BAYLER

Within your temple in this hour,
We wish to see the Human One,
To find the source of Jesus' pow'r
And witness glorious work begun.

Create in us hearts strong and pure,
And take away our grievous sin.
May life in covenant ensure
Our spirit's cleansing deep within.

As grain falls into earth to die,
To wrest new life from soil and rain,
We would the world's pretense deny
And give ourselves to Christ's domain.

We follow where our Savior leads,
Not counting either gain or loss,
Intent on meeting others' needs
Though loving all may mean a cross. Amen.

32. Come, Christ of God

Sixth Sunday of Lent—B
(Palm Sunday)

8.8.8.8. *(L.M.)*
LAVON BAYLER
(DUKE ST.)

Come, Christ of God, this is your day.
Garments are spread along your way.
With leafy branches from the field,
People respond, whom you have healed.

Come, Christ of God, the city waits;
Bring your salvation through its gates.
Blest be the One who enters here
As people shout and powers sneer.

Come, Christ of God, hosannas ring.
The temple beckons; children sing.
You have become the cornerstone
Of God's new ventures, yet unknown.

Come, Christ of God, and enter in,
Our homes to grace, our hearts to win.
Ride gently, yet with firm resolve.
Deal with our pride; our fears dissolve. Amen.

33. We Bring Our Sorrow

Sixth Sunday of Lent—B
(Passion Sunday)

8.7.8.7.
LAVON BAYLER
(RINGE RECHT)

In distress, we bring our sorrow,
Souls weighed down in misery,
Bodies wasted by our grieving,
Lives oppressed by mockery.

Whispered terror reigns around us;
Nameless fears our strength deplete.
Where is God amid this turmoil?
Where is hope to mock defeat?

God awakens, deep within us,
Ears to hear and eyes to see,
Opens us to other voices
And a new humanity.

Have the mind of Christ within you.
Jesus bore our grief and shame,
Emptied self of all pretension,
Died for us, gave us a name.

Christians, hear again the story:
Truth will reign 'gainst acts unjust.
Let your voice sustain the weary,
As they learn God's love to trust. Amen.

---

34. Steadfast Love of God

Monday of Holy Week—A,B,C

7.7.7.7.
(ST. BEES)

LAVON BAYLER

Steadfast love of God, draw near
As we face, in unknown fear,
All this week may have in store
For the Christ whom we adore.

Taking refuge 'neath God's wings,
We delight in life's good things.
Will we, then, dare venture out,
Overcoming fear and doubt?

Justice, faith, and purity
Call us forth and set us free.
In Christ's sacrifice may we
Our commissioned duties see.

Keep us faithful day by day
To the truth of Jesus' way.
May no threat'ning shadow grim
Hide Christ's light or mute our hymn. Amen.

35. O God, Our Refuge

Tuesday of Holy Week—A,B,C

8.6.8.6. (*C.M.*)
(ST. FLAVIAN)

LAVON BAYLER

O God, our refuge and our rock,
Our hope and trust from birth,
From youth to age you shelter us
And feed us from your earth.

Your foolishness calls us to life;
Your weakness makes us strong.
The cross, while folly to the wise,
Delivers us from wrong.

You rescue us from wickedness
And call us each by name.
You make our mouths as sharpened swords
Your wisdom to proclaim.

May we, as children of the light
Who follow Jesus Christ,
Be champions of love and truth
Though wealth be sacrificed.

Confirm us in our servanthood,
As Christ we glorify,
For we believe and follow One
Who, for us, chose to die. Amen.

36. Be Pleased, O God

Wednesday of Holy Week—A,B,C

8.8.8.8. (*L.M.*)
(HURSLEY)

LAVON BAYLER

Be pleased, O God, to help us now
As in your presence, we would bow
Before the One whom we betrayed,
Who, on the cross, life's sacrifice made.

May all who seek you find new joy;
May we be glad in your employ.
Sinful and needy though we be,
Fit us for your eternity.

Teach us to stand in witness true.
Open our ears to hear from you.
Save us from blows and spit and shame
That would disgrace our Savior's name.

Grant us the strength to faithful be
In service through eternity.
Equip us now for this day's task,
And grant us joy in Christ, we ask. Amen.

---

37. We Come, One Body

Maundy Thursday—B

10.10.10.10.
(EVENTIDE)

LAVON BAYLER

We come, one body, to this table spread,
Meeting the Christ, by danger buffeted.
Sharing the bread and cup before the cross,
We know once more the pain of Jesus' loss.

We have denied the One with whom we sup,
Betrayed the One who offers us the cup.
Yet Jesus breaks the bread and bids us eat,
Linking communion to God's mercy seat.

What shall we render to our God most high?
Before all people we will magnify
God's acts of mercy toward the penitent,
Joining in praise and costly covenant.

God has released us from the bonds of sin,
Called us to view all nations as our kin,
Bids us to solemn covenant be true.
All that our God has spoken, we will do. Amen.

38. My God, Why?

Good Friday—A,B,C

7.6.7.6.D.
(MUNICH)

LAVON BAYLER

My God, why have you left me,
Forsaken, far from aid?
Why am I mocked, forgotten,
Deserted, and betrayed?
I called on you to save me
From cup of suffering,
Yet sensed a larger mission
My faithfulness might bring.

Christ's sorrow and rejection
Was truly undeserved.
Christ was for us afflicted,
By taunting mobs observed.
Our weakness and transgressions
Supply the fatal nails
By which our Savior suffers
As cruel wrong prevails.

Yet still Christ's mediation
May lead us to our God,
Bring healing and forgiveness
'Long paths that Jesus trod.
For we are called disciples
And freed from guilt deserved
To work for love and justice
By which the Christ is served. Amen.

Hymns for the Easter Season

39. *Where Have They Taken Christ?*

Easter Sunday—B

10.10.10.10.
(MORECAMBE)

LAVON BAYLER

Where have they taken Christ, the Risen One?
How can we bend the knee to one unseen?
Who holds in check salvation's work begun
By Jesus Christ, the one of human mien?

No one can take triumphant life away;
Listen, and hear the Sovereign One today.
You may meet Jesus in your work or play;
Christ comes to human hearts who heed God's way.

By grace we walk, and claim our human heights,
As Jesus goes before us on life's path.
In our own Galilee the Christ invites
Good news of peace that lifts us from sin's wrath.

Come, Holy Spirit, by whom we are healed.
Come to all nations, that the world may see
God's right and truth in everyday revealed.
God's love condones no partiality. Amen.

40. *Thank You, God*

Easter Sunday—B

8.7.8.7.8.7.
(DULCE CARMEN)

LAVON BAYLER

Thank you, God, for our salvation,
Sealed in Jesus Christ today.
We have witnessed resurrection,
Know the stone was rolled away.
Halleluia! Hail our Savior,
Harbinger of God's new day!

May this day of God's own making
Cause the heavens to rejoice.
May we preach and live forgiveness,
Testify, as with one voice.
Halleluia! Saints bear witness;
We are called by God's own choice.

By God's grace we're named apostles,
By God's grace, we sing good news.
Jesus shared God's love among us,
Showed us life from diff'rent views.
Halleluia! We're disciples.
May we ne'er God's gift abuse.

Sing good news of peace among us.
Ev'ry nation bow before
God whose reconciling power
Christ has come to underscore.
Halleluia! Hail God's doing!
Sing God's praises evermore. Amen.

---

41. Who Will Roll the Stone Away?

Easter Sunday (Alternate Reading)—B

7.7.7.7.

LAVON BAYLER

(INNOCENTS)

Who will roll the stone away?
Who will comfort us today?
Jesus is not in the tomb!
Christ will e'er for us make room.

Who will take our fears away?
Who will teach us how to pray?
Jesus meets us where we are;
Help from Christ is never far.

Who will lift our sins away?
Who equip for God's new day?
Jesus lifts a peaceful goal;
Christ forgives and makes us whole.

Who will carry doubts away?
Who forever with us stay?
Jesus grants new certainty;
Christ's transforming pow'r we'll see. Amen.

42. Praise God, You Mighty Firmament

Easter Evening—B

8.6.8.6. (*C.M.*)
(ST. ANNE)

LAVON BAYLER

Praise God, you mighty firmament,
You moon and stars and sun.
Bow down in great astonishment
Before the Sovereign One.

Praise God for great and mighty deeds,
With trumpet, harp, and lute,
Raise voices high and sing your creeds
In one devout salute.

Praise God with timbrel, dance, and strings,
With pipes and cymbals loud.
As we have breath, this chorus rings:
Let everything praise God! Amen.

43. Come, Share the Joy

Easter Evening—A,B,C

7.6.7.6.D.
(ST. THEODULPH)

LAVON BAYLER

Come, share the joy of Easter,
From streets to upper room.
Some women have amazed us
With tidings from the tomb.
They say that Christ has risen
And broken death's cruel chains,
That Jesus walks among us,
And wrong no longer reigns.

High hopes for our redemption
Were shattered on the cross.
We saw no need for suff'ring
And could not deal with loss.
Such slow of heart believers,
While reasoning as fools,

We almost missed Christ's presence,
Insisting on old rules.

Did not hearts burn within us
At table with the One,
Who opened up the scriptures
Before the setting sun?
Our feet took wings, returning
To share what eyes confirmed.
The Risen One brings healing,
Forgiveness is affirmed.

To those whose eyes were blinded,
The Savior comes today.
In quiet conversation
Truth meets us on life's way.
Through breaking bread with heav'n's host
We know a joy divine.
Christ's presence opens human hearts
To love, of God's design. Amen.

---

44. We Seek to Walk in Light

Second Sunday of Easter—B

LAVON BAYLER

6.6.8.6. (S.M.)
(BOYLSTON)

We seek to walk in light
As God is in the light,
For we're united in God's truth
To try to do what's right.

We are one heart and soul,
As followers of Christ.
We testify to grace and pow'r,
By Jesus sacrificed.

We are God's partners true,
Committed to love's way,
For we have seen the risen Christ
Who brings God's fresh new day. Amen.

45. Faith in the Name of Jesus

Third Sunday of Easter—B

10.10.10.10.
(FIELD)

LAVON BAYLER

Faith in the name of Jesus makes us strong;
Christ is our life and fills our day with song.
We are God's children: loved, forgiven, blessed,
Dwelling in safety, granted peace and rest.

Why do we wonder at the power of God,
Or turn away from paths our Savior trod?
Why do we doubt the love that sets us free,
Or fail to show that love more steadily?

Lift up your light upon us, Mighty One.
Complete within us work you have begun.
Open our minds to hear your word anew.
May we respond, and to your will be true.

Times of refreshment come to us as gifts
From our Creator, who our vision lifts,
Gives us a mission, in Christ's name to preach,
That we may all the world for Jesus reach. Amen.

46. Jesus Christ Is Our Good Shepherd

Fourth Sunday of Easter—B

8.7.8.7.D.
(BEECHER)

LAVON BAYLER

Jesus Christ is our good shepherd,
Calling each of us by name,
Risking life itself to save us,
That we may our God proclaim.
We believe one flock unites us,
Though our views be different.
We are called to gather others;
On one mission we are sent.

In the Shepherd's steps we follow
By still waters, pastures green.

We are led in righteous pathways
By a rod and staff unseen.
As we walk through death's dark valley,
Evil we shall never fear,
For our Shepherd is beside us,
Always faithful, ever near.

When our enemies assail us,
When rejection we must face,
Christ anoints us with a blessing
That will many doubts erase.
Ev'ry day, with cups o'erflowing,
Good and mercy come our way.
We will dwell with God forever,
Celebrating God's new day. Amen.

---

47. Praise, All Congregations

Fifth Sunday of Easter—B

7.7.7.7.D.

LAVON BAYLER

(ST. GEORGE'S WINDSOR)

Praise, all congregations, praise
God, whose mercy crowns our days.
Hungry ones shall eat their fill,
From kind hands who do God's will.
Let us love as we've been taught,
Care for others as we ought.
God, whom we have never seen,
Promises to intervene.

Christ is God's true vine always,
Calling us to spend our days
As live branches, bearing fruits,
Anchored fully to our roots.
May God's word abide within,
Link us to our origin.
Prune us, God, that we may live
By the power you will give.

May your word be understood
By your people doing good.
Generations sing your praise

As you save from error's ways.
Your forgiveness heals, makes whole;
We respond with heart and soul
To your gift of love in One
Who eternal life has won. Amen.

---

48. Make a Joyful Noise

Sixth Sunday of Easter—B

8.6.8.6.8.6. (C.M.)
LAVON BAYLER
(CORONATION)

To God, we make a joyful noise
And sing a new, new song,
To celebrate God's faithfulness
In bringing right from wrong.
Break forth in joyous praise, all lands,
God loves us all life long.

Floods, clap your hands; hills, sing for joy
At all our God has done.
Make melody with horn and lyre
And trumpets, praising One
Who brings new birth in Jesus Christ,
God's glorious day begun.

God judges earth with righteousness,
People with equity.
Beloved children who believe
Share in the victory
By which the world is overcome
And faithful are set free.

As God loved Christ, we, too, are loved
And live by God's command.
Love one another, Jesus said,
My friends, in many lands,
My chosen and appointed ones
Through whom my work expands.

The joy of God's community
Is shared with others through

Those whom the Holy Spirit sends
Our baptism to renew.
Whate'er you ask in Jesus' name,
Our God may give to you. Amen.

---

49. When Christ Is Seen

Ascension—A,B,C
(or Seventh Sunday of Easter)

7.7.7.7.D.
(SPANISH HYMN)

LAVON BAYLER

On this day when Christ is seen
High, exalted, lifted up,
Earth and heaven in between,
We receive Christ's precious cup.
Filled with blessings from God's hand,
We respond, at Christ's command
To the One who shows us love,
Off'ring praise to God above.

Go now into all the world,
Acting on God's promises
May Christ's banner be unfurled
Through each one who practices
Jesus' care and healing pow'r.
May we worship in this hour,
Sharing in the Spirit's work
And our witness never shirk.

Questions do not overwhelm
Those who praise God's majesty
Knowing seasons of God's realm
Fixed by God's authority.
Ours is, rather, to give thanks
Serving God within the ranks
Of apostles, filled with zeal,
Praying we may Christ reveal. Amen.

50. Grant Us Your Joy

6.6.4.6.6.6.4.

LAVON BAYLER

(CUTTING)

Grant us your joy today;
May we be one, we pray,
Living your word.
As Christ our hope revives,
We consecrate our lives,
Knowing your truth survives,
Often unheard.

Grant us your joy today;
May we be one, we pray,
For Jesus' sake.
Guided by Christ, whose way
Keeps us from going astray,
Building the better day,
We'll undertake.

Grant us your joy today;
May we be one, we pray.
Both aged and youth.
Keep us within your love;
May we find strength thereof,
Lifting our eyes above,
Searching for truth.

Grant us your joy today;
May we be one, we pray,
Yielding good fruit.
May we apostles be,
Delight your law to see,
Sharing in ministry,
Evil refute. Amen.

Hymns for the Pentecost Season

51. On This Day of Expectation

Pentecost Sunday—B

8.7.8.7.D.
(HYMN TO JOY)

LAVON BAYLER

On this day of expectation
When your Spirit fills our hearts,
We become a new creation
In the strength your breath imparts.
Come again, and bless all nations,
Joining all our aged and youth
In your joyous celebrations,
Guiding us to know your truth.

Knit our dry bones back together;
Grant our flesh to know rebirth.
May we live in you forever,
As you give our lives new worth.
Stand us on our feet, rejoicing,
Singing praise for all your gifts,
With each breath devotion voicing,
As your truth the church uplifts.

Send your Counselor forever,
God of mighty wind and fire.
Grant that we may hear, and never
Lesser messages desire.
Fill us now with expectation
As your glory we perceive.
Speak to ev'ry heart and nation;
May we all your word receive. Amen.

52. Holy, Holy, Holy God

Trinity Sunday—B

7.6.7.6.D.
(ST. KEVIN)

LAVON BAYLER

Holy, holy, holy God,
Author of creation,
Earth proclaims your glorious strength
And your great salvation.
Mighty winds and flames evoke
Songs of adoration,
As we join your family
In this celebration.

Woe is me, for I am lost,
Who shall come to save me?
Who will purge my unclean lips
And release from slav'ry?
How can we be born anew,
Leaving past attractions?
Jesus Christ, God's Human One,
Conquers our distractions.

When the Holy Spirit comes,
Thund'ring 'cross the waters,
Or as gentle as a breath,
To God's sons and daughters,
All our guilt is swept away
And our sins forgiven,
We respond in grateful praise,
Singing, "Christ is risen."

God so loved the world, and us,
That, no cost withholding,
One was sent to bear our sins,
Fuller life unfolding.
We can only speak with joy
As we tell our story;
Though, with Christ, we suffer now,
Still, we see God's glory. Amen.

53. Great God, We Bring

Pentecost 2—B

8.6.8.6.D. *(C.M.D.)*
LAVON BAYLER (MATERNA)

Great God, we bring our hearts' desire
Before your majesty,
To seek your help for humankind,
Bowed down in misery.
To those afflicted but uncrushed,
Struck down but not destroyed,
You grant the power of your love
E'en yet to be enjoyed.

You answer when we pray to you,
Though we may not discern
The good you offer on our way
Or truth you'd have us learn.
While we observe appearances
And status wealth imparts,
You do not see as people see,
For you behold our hearts.

O God, as days of trouble come,
Send light upon our path,
That we may know the strength of Christ
To save from evil's wrath.
Grant knowledge of your glory now,
And melt each hardened soul.
Stretch out your hand with healing love
To change us and console. Amen.

54. Grace Extends to All

Pentecost 3—B

8.7.8.7.D.
LAVON BAYLER (AUSTRIAN HYMN)

Grace extends to all your people,
God of love and faithfulness,

So we worship 'neath the steeple,
Gathered by your holiness.
We do not lose heart or waver,
Growing older day by day,
For we know your boundless favor
Brings renewal on life's way.

Now exalted in the heavens,
God, your glory shines on earth.
We, with souls bowed down, but steadfast,
Sing our songs to praise your worth.
You compel our admiration
With the marvels we have seen.
How much more, among the nations,
We extol those things unseen.

May your music swell within us,
As your whole creation sings.
We take refuge from destruction
In the shadow of your wings.
We would turn from all divisions,
As you take us by the hand.
Knowing we have been forgiven,
We have confidence to stand. Amen.

---

55. Be Still and Know

Pentecost 4—B

8.8.8.8. (L.M.)
LAVON BAYLER   (FEDERAL STREET)

Be still and know that God is God,
Greater than we will ever know,
Leading us where our Savior trod,
Granting us strength in Christ to grow.

Take courage, then, by faith to walk
Throughout this earth we call our home.
Christ is our pattern as we talk,
Present to guide where'er we roam.

May all we do reflect Christ's love,
Who died for all that we might live.
No human plan, or view thereof,
Leads us so selflessly to give.

Living for others is our aim,
As selfless service fills each day.
God's new creation we would claim,
Giving ourselves to Jesus' way. Amen.

---

56. *Walking by Faith*

Pentecost 4—B

6.6.4.6.6.4.
(CUTTING)

LAVON BAYLER

Walking by faith, not sight,
We in God's world delight,
Living in awe.
God sends the sun and rain,
Granting us fruit and grain,
Pointing to Jesus' reign
Within God's law.

Walking by faith, not sight,
We come to Jesus' light
In growing trust.
Gone are our yesterdays
And all our selfish ways.
Christ sets our hearts ablaze
For causes just.

Walking by faith, not sight,
We pray to do what's right
As nations rage.
God overcomes our fears,
Breaking our bows and spears
'Til warfare disappears
In God's new age. Amen.

57. Amid the Storms

Pentecost 5—B

8.8.8.8. *(L.M.)*
(OLIVE'S BROW)

LAVON BAYLER

Amid the storms along life's way,
When we encounter threats and fear,
The One whom wind and sea obey
Discerns our need and draws us near.

We hear the wind rebuked, in awe
At Jesus' calming, "Peace, be still."
In faith that goes beyond the law,
We dare to seek our Savior's will.

Through Christ we know salvation now
Within this present time and space.
God helps and listens when we bow
Before abiding love and grace.

We have been reconciled to God
By Christ who takes away our sin.
Ambassadors where Christ has trod,
We lead friends to their Origin.

What we have heard and seen, we share,
That all may know God's steadfast love.
As we enjoy God's gracious care,
Our praises soar to heights above. Amen.

58. O Strong and Mighty God

Pentecost 6—B

11.10.11.10.11.10.
(FINLANDIA)

LAVON BAYLER

O strong and mighty God, our Glor'ous Ruler,
We stand in awe before your pow'r today.
As faith and trust surmount the fears within us,
You lead our feet to follow your high way.
Free us to lift our voices, harps, and cymbals,
To sing your praise and celebrate life's goals.

All earth is yours, O God of all creation;
The fullness of the land and sea are yours.
We look to mountains in their tow'ring grandeur,
The holy places where your word endures.
O, wash our hands and cleanse our hearts within us,
That we may live your purpose glorious.

We know your grace, poured out in great abundance,
In Christ who left the riches of your realm,
To live among the poor along earth's byways,
Revealing love, lest evil overwhelm.
O, let us know your healing touch and presence,
That we may rise in helpful reverence. Amen.

---

59. God of Our Parents

Pentecost 7—B

LAVON BAYLER

10.10.10.10.
(LANGRAN)

God of our parents, you have been our guide
Through all life's torments, always at our side.
Your steadfast love is everywhere at hand,
And when we pray, we know you understand.

You have been with us in our joy and pain,
With grace and pow'r sufficient to sustain
And to perfect us for our ministry
As your disciples, seeking unity.

You take our weaknesses and make us strong,
Helping us know to whom our lives belong,
Drawing us into covenant, by grace,
Off'ring to heal us in your warm embrace.

Move us beyond our self-protective schemes
To follow Christ, who daily life redeems.
Joining in faithful witness, we will dare
Not just to speak, but honestly to care. Amen.

60. Your Word Is True, O God

Pentecost 8—B

6.6.8.6 *(S.M.)*

LAVON BAYLER

(FESTAL SONG)

Your word is true, O God;
Your promises prevail.
We seek your blessing for our homes,
That love may never fail.

Your covenant calls forth
The best we have within,
Awakening our spirits' depths
And saving us from sin.

You satisfy the poor
With bread enough to eat,
And dwell among us with your grace
That we, with joy, now greet.

As your adopted ones,
We know ourselves set free,
Redeemed, forgiven, and empow'red,
To serve humanity.

We seek to do your will,
Revealed through history,
Uniting earth and heav'n in Christ,
Your perfect mystery.

Grant wisdom when we go
To journey in Christ's name,
That we may use authority
Your healing to proclaim. Amen.

---

61. Deliver Us, Most Gracious God

Pentecost 9—B

8.6.8.6. *(C.M.)*

LAVON BAYLER

(DUNDEE)

Deliver us, most gracious God,
From attitudes that kill,

From evil works that have no place
Within your sovereign will.

Save us, we pray, from selfish acts
That say, "God doesn't care,"
From using people day by day
In ways that are unfair.

Release us from corrupt intent,
Depravity, and sin.
O, may we not be put to shame
But find new life within.

Help us, O God, to understand
Your ways are not our own.
Reject us not when we have strayed
And leave us not alone.

Restore in us a sense of hope;
Renew our confidence,
That we may learn and teach with joy
Your great deliverance. Amen.

---

62. Christ Is Our Perfect Peace

Pentecost 9—B
Based on Ephesians 2:11–22

6.4.6.5.6.6.6.5.
(BETHANY)

LAVON BAYLER

Christ is our perfect peace,
Who made us one,
Renewing hope within
Promises begun.
  Refrain:
  As one humanity,
  We dwell in unity
  From all hostility
  Rescued and set free.

By Christ's pure sacrifice,
We are brought near
To One Eternal God
We no longer fear.
  Refrain

Strangers no longer, we
Dwell with the saints,
Living in covenant,
Freed by love's restraints.
   Refrain

Christ is the cornerstone;
We are the church,
Built on the prophets' word
And apostles' search.
   Refrain

May we Christ's temple be,
Living in peace,
Working for justice and
Spiritual release.
   Refrain
Amen.

---

63. *How Have We Despised Your Word?*

Pentecost 10—B

7.7.7.7.7.7.
(AJALON)

LAVON BAYLER

How have we despised your word,
God of loving amnesty?
How have we, with scorn, misused
Your creation's majesty?
Hear us as we now confess
All the guilt that brings distress.

God, convict us of our sin;
Rescue us from greed's assaults.
Help us see the wrong we've done;
Turn us from unconscious faults.
Hear us as we now declare
Our intent to serve with care.

Blessed are we who, sin confessed,
Find new strength and confidence,
Knowing we have been forgiv'n,
Rising from our punishments.

Teach us, God, with eyes on you,
How to trust your word so true.

Move us from our stubbornness
And from visions limited.
May our prayers embrace your world,
All of earth's discomfited.
Teach us to rejoice and give
Gladness and the will to live. Amen.

---

64. We Cry to You, Creator

Pentecost 11—B

LAVON BAYLER

7.6.7.6.D.
(ANGEL'S STORY)

We cry to you, Creator;
You know our troubled days.
Your ears are tuned to hear us;
Your eyes behold our ways.
When we are brokenhearted
And angry and distraught,
You grieve with us and offer
The peace that we have sought.

Your face is set 'gainst evil,
Though we deny your good.
You granted bread from heaven
Which we misunderstood.
Afflictions of the righteous
Were lifted on the cross
By Christ who bore our sorrow,
Our evil, pain, and loss.

Now we believe the promise
That life will be renewed,
For we have heard you calling
When we our hopes pursued.
In lowliness and meekness,
Forbearing all with love,
We seek your Spirit's oneness
And power from above.

United in one baptism,
One Lord, one faith for all,
We seek the living water
That is continual.
May all whose spirits hunger
Discover living bread
And know your Spirit's leading
By which our souls are fed. Amen.

---

65. Hear All Our Prayers

Pentecost 12—B

LAVON BAYLER

8.8.8.8. *(L.M.)*
(PENTECOST)

Hear all our prayers, O Sovereign God;
Teach us the way that we should go.
Give ear to all that we confess;
That your forgiveness we may know.

Take all that's evil from our mouths
And from our attitudes and acts.
Forgive our sin, and guilt remove;
Grant now the love your servant lacks.

You offer bread of life, made known
In Jesus Christ, through whom we trust
Your all-compelling will and way,
Urging concern for causes just.

Write on our hearts the good we know;
Carve your directions on our days,
That we may know as we are known,
And follow truth in all our ways. Amen.

66. O God, as We Come

8.6.8.6.D. (C.M.D.)

LAVON BAYLER

(ST. LEONARD)

O God, as we, your children, come
To know the love you give,
We ask to have the mind of Christ
That we may truly live.
As Jesus gave up life for us,
A fragrant offering,
We dare to speak of sacrifice
While risking everything.

Direct our anger into good,
Remove our wrath and pain;
May malice and all bitterness
Ne'er be our life's refrain.
Turn us away from evil talk
And let us speak with grace.
May honest labor fit us to
Improve the commonplace.

Uplifting one another's good,
We would be kind and true,
Reflecting God's forgiving love
In all we say and do.
In tenderhearted friendliness,
We sense our neighbors' need
And imitate God's gracious care
As their concerns we heed. Amen.

67. Make Melody to God

6.6.8.6. (S.M.)

LAVON BAYLER

(TRENTHAM)

Make melody to God
With all your heart today.

Always, for ev'rything, give thanks;
God hears us when we pray.

Cry out in your distress;
God will incline an ear,
Speedily answer when you call,
And banish doubt and fear.

Be careful how you walk,
Making the most of time,
Seeking to understand God's will
And know God's love sublime.

Christ is the living bread
Sent down from heav'n for you,
That anyone who eats may live
Forever, strong and true. Amen.

---

68. God, Who Dawns as Morning

Pentecost 14—B

7.7.7.7.7.7.
(PILOT)

LAVON BAYLER

God, who dawns as morning light,
Like the sun when skies are bright,
Shine on us and show your way,
As you lead us through this day.
May we in your word delight,
God, who dawns as morning light.

God, whose wisdom sends the rain,
Making grass spring from the plain,
Seal us in your covenant,
That no woes may disenchant.
May we worship you aright,
God, who dawns as morning light.

Living God, who sends us bread,
That by Christ we may be fed,
Keep us faithful, keep us just,
As we learn in you to trust.
We your gracious deeds recite,
God, who dawns as morning light.

Let all nations sing for joy
And their energy employ,
In obedience to your will,
Peaceful purposes fulfill.
Grant your grace, renew our sight,
That the world may know your light. Amen.

---

69. Lift Up Your Eyes

Pentecost 15—B

LAVON BAYLER

8.6.8.6.8.6. (C.M.)
(CORONATION)

Lift up your eyes unto the hills
And seek the help of God,
That you may live the life God wills
And walk where Jesus trod,
Employing all the peaceful skills
With which your feet are shod.

God is the keeper of your life,
The shade on your right hand,
Your helper in the midst of strife,
Your armor, to withstand
The evil days when sin is rife,
Defiling all the land.

This day, through Christ, stand straight and strong
In righteousness and praise,
Receiving truth to save from wrong
And set your spirits ablaze.
May all of life to God belong
In service all your days.

With all your heart and soul today
Go forth in faithfulness.
By God's command, in Jesus' way,
Be strong and courageous,
In all you think and do and say
That God may surely bless. Amen.

70. Every Gift and Good Endowment

Pentecost 16—B

8.7.8.7.
(STUTTGART)

LAVON BAYLER

Every gift and good endowment
Comes from you, O God of light,
For our wisdom and enjoyment
As we walk by faith and sight.

Heal our brokenness and deafness
That we may be quick to hear.
May our souls respond with meekness
And with faith to persevere.

Keep us from deceit and anger;
Let no evil overcome.
Turn us from all false religion
To a faith more venturesome.

We receive your words of promise,
Treasuring your firm command.
We would serve in awe and wonder,
Confident you understand.

May our work reflect your justice
And your law of liberty.
May our witness move your people
To renewed integrity. Amen.

71. Come, Sisters and Brothers

Pentecost 17—B

11.11.11.11.
(ST. DENIO)

LAVON BAYLER

Come, sisters and brothers, to join us in song,
For God is our refuge, who saves us from wrong.
God welcomes all people, the rich and the poor,
Both faithful and sinner, both young and mature.

Those giving their bounty to meet others' need,
While working for justice and turning from greed,
Shall find true fulfillment in God's holy law,
In loving of neighbor and serving with awe.

The upright of heart shall know goodness inside;
Those trusting in God shall forever abide.
Disciples denying themselves for a cross
And risking their lives shall not know death as loss. Amen.

---

72. For the Poor

Pentecost 17—B

8.7.8.7.D.
(ERIE)

LAVON BAYLER

For the poor whom you have chosen,
We implore your help today.
God of every age and people,
Hear the needy when they pray.
We acknowledge Christ among us,
Prompting faith and works as one;
When we see injustice, wake us,
That through us your will be done.

We confess that we have failed you
With distinctions that deny
Equal worth of all your children
And the promise you supply.
We have chosen to be partial
Toward the ones more finely clothed
While your care is for the hungry
And the weak whom we have loathed.

May we never say to others,
"Go in peace; be warmed and filled,"
While we fail to ease their hunger
Or their confidence rebuild.
Turn us from our crooked pathways
To the goodness you intend;
May we share the wealth you've given
And our selfishness transcend.

As your Human One has suffered

To redeem us from our sin,
May we give ourselves for others
And reclaim our origin.
You have made us to be lovers
Who from pain will not withdraw.
Help us stand with all your people
To uphold your royal law. Amen.

---

73. Why Did We Talk of Rank?

Pentecost 18—B

8.6.8.6. (C.M.)
(FINGAL)

LAVON BAYLER

Why did we talk along the road
Of greatness, pow'r, and rank?
In wisdom, God our gifts bestowed;
Now God we pause to thank.

All those who first position seek
No privilege deserve;
While each one is to God unique,
We all must learn to serve.

There is no place for jealousy
Or arrogant pretense
Among the folks from sin set free
By gracious Providence.

We see God's love personified
In children's perfect trust.
O, may we in such faith abide
That we become more just.

Let gentleness and mercy reign,
With wisdom from above,
That, healing one another's pain,
Our lives may know God's love. Amen.

74. Be Patient as You Wait

Pentecost 19—B

8.6.8.6.D. (C.M.D.)
(GENEVA)

LAVON BAYLER

Be patient as you wait for God
Whose purposes are sure.
Be strong, take courage, lift your hearts;
God's goodness will endure
Through times of loss and violence,
False witness and despair.
Though all forsake, God takes us up
In love and gentle care.

No matter what tomorrow brings,
Find purpose in today,
For you can trust the Sovereign One
To guide you on the way.
God will not hide or turn from you
When times are at their worst
Nor when you grumble and complain
And feel that you are cursed.

The God of our salvation hears
And answers when we call.
God gives us mighty works to do
As servants, one and all.
As salty Christians, reaching out
To season life with care,
Give cups of water lovingly
And peace for all to share. Amen.

75. Blessed Are the Ones

Pentecost 20—B

10.10.10.10.
(SONG 24)

LAVON BAYLER

Blessed are the ones who their Creator praise,
And live in awe while walking in God's ways.

In Jesus Christ we form one family,
Sisters and brothers seeking harmony.

We have one Origin who sanctifies,
Who hears our prayer and every good supplies.
O, worship God, by whom all things exist,
Sing of God's glory and by faith persist.

From the beginning, we in God abide,
Called to be partners, working side by side,
Sharing commitments and fidelity
Toward Jesus' goal of perfect unity.

May all your children learn your way of peace
And in your love find meaningful release.
Lifted by grace to our salvation claim,
May we forevermore extol your name. Amen.

---

76. Grant Sabbath Rest

Pentecost 21—B

8.8.8.8. *(L.M.)*
LAVON BAYLER   (CANONBURY)

Grant sabbath rest, O gracious God,
For all who love and seek your truth.
May your good news be read and heard
This day by women, men, and youth.

Let not your anger overwhelm
Or wrath consume your people here.
Incline our hearts to seek your realm
Where poor are rich, as Christ made clear.

How, sharper than a two-edged sword,
Your word cuts through walls that divide,
Evoking faith and true accord
As we our inmost thoughts confide.

The sin we seek to hide from view
Is soon revealed within your light.
May your forgiveness now renew
The promises our words recite. Amen.

77. What Shall We Do, O Christ?

Pentecost 21—B

6.6.8.6. *(S.M.)*
(LAKE ENON)

LAVON BAYLER

What shall we do, O Christ,
To know eternal life?
For we are by our wealth enticed
To self-protective strife.

We would not kill or steal,
Defraud or cheat or lie.
Devotion in our homes is real,
Your truth we'll not deny.

Now, by your word dismayed,
We hear our wealth attacked.
Demands of Christ find us afraid.
To dare what we have lacked.

How shall we give away
The substance that supplies
The things we need for every day,
On which all life relies?

No needle offers space
To let a camel through
Who will be saved if there is place
For just a gen'rous few?

Lead us where Christ has trod,
Astonished by the word:
"All things are possible with God;
Your prayers are always heard."

All that we risk for you
Has by your love been giv'n.
Eternal life will see us through
Earth's troubles into heav'n.

O God, who grants all good,
While giving us commands,
May your desires be understood,
Your work engage our hands. Amen.

78. Hear Us, O God

Pentecost 22—B

10.10.10.10.
(ELLERS)

LAVON BAYLER

Hear us, O God, when we are sore distressed,
Unfairly stricken, wrongfully oppressed.
God, be not silent as your servants bear
Sham and deceit when no one seems to care.

Rescue your people from temptation's snare;
Stoop to our weakness with your loving care.
Save us from pride and arrogant pretense;
Help us to serve with Christ-like confidence.

Hear now our thanks for grace in time of need
As your forgiveness makes us rich indeed.
Clothe us with righteousness and bring us peace
Through Christ, whose sacrifice won our release.

God, make us able now to face our foes
Who speak against us, adding to our woes.
Lift us from weakness to your Spirit's pow'r
That we may know fulfillment hour by hour. Amen.

79. O, Sing Aloud

Pentecost 23—B

8.6.8.6. *(C.M.)*
(ST. PETER)

LAVON BAYLER

O, sing aloud with grateful joy,
God's blessing to proclaim
God saves the people from their sins
And gathers blind and lame.

Those weeping find new confidence,
The hurting claim true joy,
For God consoles and leads us back
To gifts we may employ.

We celebrate our great High Priest
Who acts on our behalf,
Deals gently with our ignorance
And teaches us to laugh.

O, follow, then, in Jesus' way
Where blind receive their sight.
May others find their faith made strong
As we to Christ invite. Amen.

---

80. We Love You, Christ

Pentecost 24—B

LAVON BAYLER

7.6.7.6.D.
(WEBB)

We love you, Christ, our Savior,
Our great High Priest above,
For you have died for sinners
And rescued us in love.
Your sacrifice and off'ring
Made once to draw us all
To God, our great Creator:
In you, we hear God's call.

In love, you summoned Israel,
And call to us today,
Inviting hearts to love you
And follow Jesus' way.
With soul and mind we honor
Your claims upon our strength,
Devote ourselves completely,
Go with you any length.

Your love is first within us;
We love our neighbor, too.
The second great commandment
Keeps others' needs in view
And calls for our attention
To worth that you entrust
To each of us, your children,
Formed by you out of dust.

In loving selves and others,
Our love for you grows strong;
Your promises sustain us
Through all the ages long.
Incline our hearts to trust you
As all your law we keep,
As, serving one another,
Our lives true freedom reap. Amen.

---

81. We Trust, O God, in You

Pentecost 25—B

6.6.8.6.D. (S.M.D.)
(LEOMINSTER)

LAVON BAYLER

We trust, O God, in you,
Our helper and our hope,
To grant to us the larger view
As with today we cope.
When problems overwhelm
And human recourse fails,
We know ourselves within your realm
And pray your will prevails.

Your praise, O God, we sing;
Your justice we proclaim.
The hungry eat the food you bring;
You save the weak from shame.
You open blinded eyes
And set the pris'ner free;
Your faithful caring magnifies
The goodness that we see

Keep us from false pretense,
And seeking our own gain.
May faith outrun experience
And make us more humane.
Your generosity
Has prompted us to share;
The widow, in her poverty,
Has taught us how to care.

When we are filled with fear
Amid uncertainties,
Your reassuring word we hear
That bears us up and frees.
Your love has given breath;
To love we shall return,
When life's short journey, closed by death,
Brings peace for which we yearn. Amen.

82. Proclaim the Glorious Splendor

Pentecost 26—B

10.10.10.10.

LAVON BAYLER   (TOULON)

Proclaim the glorious splendor of God's reign.
Speak of a power we cannot explain.
Make known the mighty deeds of One whose grace
Offers forgiveness and a growing place.

Faithful in covenant, our God provides
Loving compassion which through time abides,
Prompting our thanks for all God's grace imparts,
Writing eternal law on minds and hearts.

Come in dominion, Human One, Divine,
That we, in you, may with God's glory shine.
Offering day by day, in word and deed,
Clear demonstration of our faith and creed. Amen.

83. In These Days

Pentecost 26—B

8.7.8.7.

LAVON BAYLER   (GALILEE)

In these days of tribulation
When the stars begin to fall,

When the sun and moon are darkened,
God of mercy, hear our call.

When your judgment falls upon us
In the treachery of sin,
Send your light and your salvation;
Touch our spirits deep within.

Reign o'er us in glorious splendor,
God of grace and steadfast love,
May your realm be known among us;
Lift our vision high above.

In your mercy and compassion,
Grant us vision for our days.
May your Holy Spirit lead us
In your covenant always. Amen.

---

84. Your Reign, O God

Pentecost 27—B

8.6.8.6. *(C.M.)*
(ST. ANNE)

LAVON BAYLER

Your reign, O God, shall never end,
Nor origin reveal,
For your almighty purposes
Are far beyond time's weal.

Your voice, like mighty thunder sounds;
The waves upon the seas
Proclaim your holiness to all
Who seek your sure decrees.

Our Alpha and Omega, God
of righteousness and peace,
We dwell securely in the hope
Your love shall never cease.

That love, revealed in Jesus Christ,
Stands up to earthly power.
It reigns beyond all time and space
And holds this present hour.

So gather now, as remnant, all
Devoted to your truth,
That we may rise with Christ, renewed
To serve, as vibrant youth.

Equip the shepherds of your flock
That they may ne'er destroy
The faith of those within their care,
But multiply true joy. Amen.

Hymns for Other Special Occasions

85. We Hear Your Messenger

Presentation (February 2)—A, B, C

LAVON BAYLER

6.6.8.6. (S.M.)
(ST. ANDREW)

We hear your messenger,
Come like refiner's fire
To purify our offerings
And fill our heart's desire.

How lovely where you dwell;
'Tis here we long to stay,
For you provide the strength we need
To face life day by day.

This house of prayer and praise
Is where we sing for joy.
To you, the living God most high,
Who would our lips employ.

Christ blessed our human life
By birth in human form,
Destroying death, affirming truth,
Of which Christ was the norm.

Let us depart in peace,
According to your word,
That we may Christ's salvation share,
As we have seen and heard. Amen.

86. We Are Your People

Annunciation (March 25)—A, B, C

LAVON BAYLER

8.5.8.5.
(CAIRNBROOK)

We are your own, favored people,
Knowing you are near.
We have heard your quiet summons,
And we will not fear.

In your Holy Spirit's power,
We have confidence;
Nothing is impossible in
Your great providence.

We will not resort to testing
For some feeble signs,
But announce your great deliv'rance,
Which to us inclines.

As of old you came to Mary,
Come with news for us,
May the Child whom Mary mothered
Lead our exodus.

When we bring ourselves as off'rings,
We know you will bless.
We would give our best in service,
In true eagerness. Amen.

---

87. My Heart Exults in God

Visitation (May 31)—A, B, C

LAVON BAYLER

8.8.8.8. *(L.M.)*
(SAXBY)

My heart exults in God, my rock;
God takes my strength and lifts it up.
I will rejoice, 'mid those who mock,
Sharing my home and loaf and cup.

May love be genuine indeed;
Hold fast to what is good and true;
Contribute to the saints in need;
Show one another honor too.

Hate what is evil in God's sight
But do not curse those doing wrong.
Bless those who persecute and fight;
They, too, are kin, to God belong.

In tribulation, patient be;
Rejoice with those who celebrate.
Offer your hospitality
And with the poor associate.

Rejoice in hope, be strong in prayer;
Glow with the Spirit; serve with zeal.
When others weep, be there to care;
In friendship, share what others feel.

Praise God forever, come what may;
God's mighty actions, now acclaim.
Through our distress, God points the way;
Sing to God's glory, bless God's name. Amen.

---

88. God of Mystery and Grace

Holy Cross (September 14)—A, B, C

7.7.7.7.7.7.
(TOPLADY)

LAVON BAYLER

God of mystery and grace,
As we humbly seek your face,
We admit our doubts and fears,
That have plagued us through the years.
We have stumbled o'er the cross,
Seeing only pain and loss.

We confess that we have sought
To be clever, with no thought
That the ways of God alone
Hold the wisdom we've not known.
From our foolishness we reach
For the truth disciples preach.

Your forgiveness turns our wrong
To salvation, making strong
Our return to covenant.
Make our lives more radiant,
As your wisdom and your pow'r
Shape new life in us this hour.

Help us sing of victory
That in Christ has set us free
From the lies your truth destroys.
May we make a joyful noise,
Praising you for ending strife,
Granting us eternal life. Amen.

89. Saints, Rejoice and Sing

***All Saints (November 1,
or first Sunday in November)—B***

LAVON BAYLER

7.8.7.8.7.7.
(RATISBON)

Saints, behold God's dwelling place,
With humanity residing,
Reigning over time and space,
Yet within each one abiding.
God is with us through our days;
Saints, rejoice and sing God's praise.

All the earth our Maker claims,
Making new all things within it.
All who dwell therein, God names,
Knowing what we do each minute.
God forgives each one who strays;
Saints, rejoice and sing God's praise.

Hail the new Jerusalem,
Where no pain or death or mourning,
Join in heaven's requiem,
Former ways of falsehood scorning.
Alpha and Omega raise;
Saints, rejoice and sing God's praise.

Purify our hands and hearts
To ascend your holy mountain,
Knowing that your love imparts
Blessings far beyond our counting.
We give thanks for all your ways;
Saints, rejoice and sing God's praise.

Now we pray to do your will;
Fill us with your strength and power.
May we bear good fruit, and still
Seek more challenge for each hour.
For endurance God conveys,
Saints, rejoice and sing God's praise. Amen.

226   Hymns for Other Special Occasions

90. God, We Rejoice

Thanksgiving Day—B

10.10.10.10.
(NATIONAL HYMN)

LAVON BAYLER

God, we rejoice, for you have done great things;
All of creation with your goodness rings.
Pastures and vines and trees all give full yield;
Harvests of gold, your mercy has revealed.

Sunshine and rain have blessed our fertile land;
Vats overflow with bounty from your hand.
'Round us is plenty, meant for us to share
With needy people, here and everywhere.

Yet, in our panic and anxiety,
We wonder what our source of food will be
If things go wrong and future ventures fail.
God, may abundance in all lands prevail!

Think of the birds, which never sow or reap,
Or of the lilies, which no wardrobes keep.
Think how much more our God for us provides;
Do not be anxious, God with us abides.

Let thanks ring out in shouts and prayers and praise
To our Creator through the coming days.
Grant us your peace and quiet godliness,
As your salvation's joy we all confess. Amen.

91. Praise Be to God

Baptism, Communion

10.10.10.10.
(NATIONAL HYMN)

LAVON BAYLER

Praise be to God, from whom all life has come,
Whose great commandments are not burdensome.
Baptized and called by God to ministry,
We would, at table, find community.

We celebrate the baptism we share,

Christ's death and resurrection to declare.
Joining our Savior in a life made new,
We show God's glory in all things we do.

In our communion at Christ's table spread,
We share the mystery of wine and bread.
One in Christ's body, seeking unity,
Subdue, we pray, the ways we disagree.

We have this ministry of love and grace,
God's saving action through all life to trace.
Called out, forgiven, reconciled, set free,
In humble wonder, we God's reign foresee. Amen.

---

92. Ministers by God's Grace

Ministry

8.6.8.6. *(C.M.)*
(ST. ANNE)

LAVON BAYLER

As ministers by God's own grace,
Committed messengers,
We share good news in ev'ry place,
Then serve as listeners.

As ministers of Jesus Christ,
We preach and teach and heal,
Embracing life, once sacrificed,
Forgiveness to reveal.

As ministers who, Spirit-filled,
Proclaim love's saving pow'r,
We seek community to build
To serve this present hour.

As ministers of God triune,
We sing our Maker's praise,
As with the Spirit we commune
And follow Jesus' ways. Amen.

93. We Praise You, Creator

Ministry

LAVON BAYLER

11.11.11.11.
(ST. DENIO)

We praise you, Creator of all time and space,
For gifts of the Spirit, received by your grace.
All wisdom and healing and tongues set on fire
Are given the whole of your church to inspire.

Your spirit has granted for our common good
All talents, so varied and misunderstood.
While one is a prophet, another will teach;
One serves you with actions, another with speech.

Interpreters, helpers, administrators,
All miracle workers, all faithful pastors,
Are part of your varied and wonderful plan
Of interdependence since time first began.

We gather, one body, as we're meant to be.
While one part is hearing, another will see.
A hand cannot say, "I have no need of you,"
To feet that support us and carry us through.

We serve you, Creator of all of our days,
Employing your gifts in a myriad of ways.
Inspire all our efforts and help us to be
Your faithful apostles, in strong unity. Amen.

94. Creator, Bless These Loved Ones*

Farewell Hymn

LAVON BAYLER

7.6.7.6.D.
(LANCASHIRE)

Creator, bless these loved ones
Who travel far away,
And grant them your protection
For ev'ry passing day.
Our thoughts and prayers go with them

In challenges they face.
Equip them for new ventures;
Empow'r them by your grace.

Our lives have known their caring
In times of work and play.
Now we will miss their presence
And all they have to say.
Lord, help us fill the silence
Which their departure brings.
Uplift our fallen spirits
And give our hopes new wings.

Unite us in your service
'Cross miles that separate;
Expand our gifts and sharing
That we may demonstrate
In all our thoughts and actions
Our reach for truth above.
Refresh us by your Spirit
To serve your world with love. Amen.

*Written in honor of "Clip" and Janice Higgins.

---

95. Celebrate God's Love*

Installation Hymn

8.7.8.7.D.
(HYMN TO JOY)

LAVON BAYLER

Celebrate God's love among us
Calling us to claim this day
For the future of our churches
And the reign of Jesus' way.
Christ our Savior journeys with us
In new ventures yet unthought,
Promising to love and guide us
Through new paths where we'll be taught.

Celebrate our new beginnings
In a partnership of trust
May God's all-transcending presence
Help us all to readjust
To the broad, exciting vision

Christ would set before us now.
May the covenant we enter
All with hope and love endow.

Celebrate the gifts so varied
Which the Spirit will provide.
Join each other in the mission
That is local and worldwide.
May the Spirit now uplift us
As we face the future days,
With integrity and caring
And in mutual prayer and praise. Amen.

*Written for the installation of the Rev. Clarence M. "Clip" Higgins Jr. as Conference Minister of the Nebraska Conference UCC.

96. Most Gracious God*

Honoring Pastors

8.6.8.8.6.

LAVON BAYLER   (REST)

Most gracious God, whose deeds we praise,
Accept the thanks we bring
For pastors who live out your ways.
Hear now the gratitude we raise
As joyously we sing.

We thank you for the truth-filled word
Our minister proclaims.
By sermons bold our hearts are stirred;
In caring acts your love is heard
Through one who knows our names.

We celebrate the faithfulness
Of one who does not shirk
The daily labors that express
A trust in your intent to bless
Disciple's selfless work.

We, too, would die to self to live
According to your will.
We honor your imperative
To follow Christ, ourselves to give,
Your purpose to fulfill. Amen.

*Written for the 30th ordination anniversary of the Rev. William L. Nagy.

97. God, Who Blessed Us*

Church Centennial

8.7.8.7.D.
(HYMN TO JOY)

LAVON BAYLER

God, who blessed us for a cent'ry,
Fill our hearts with love today.
Turn our deeds to serve you only;
Fix our thoughts upon your way.
You have led our parents forward
Through all wars and human strife,
May our children hail your standard
As their guide for all of life.

You have seen Christ's cup before us,
Know it speaks of suffering.
Where we seize it just for status,
Turn it to an offering.
We've enlisted in the service
Of the One from Galilee.
We will work for human justice
That God's children may be free.

Teach us, in this celebration,
How to fight the fight of faith;
Where to make our affirmation
'Gainst all jealousy and hate.
Grant us patience and endurance,
Love and faith and gentleness.
As God gives in rich abundance,
May we share with eagerness.

As foundation for the future
God has called us to be good.
Not for pride or ego's nurture
Do we do the things we should.
Rather, to God's greatest glory
Will we serve both aged and youth.
Let our actions tell the story
Of the Christ whose life was truth. Amen.

*Written for the 100th anniversary observance of St. Paul United Church of Christ, Hinckley, Illinois.

98. On This, Our Day of Days

Wedding Service

LAVON BAYLER

6.6.6.6.6.6.
(LAUDES DOMINI)

O God, whose love and care
Surrounds us everywhere,
We bring our joy and praise.
May we your presence know
Within the wedding glow
On this, our day of days.

For family and friends
And love that never ends
We bring our joy and praise.
May happiness abound
With each delightful sound
On this, our day of days.

As you, O God, forgive
And teach us how to live,
We bring our joy and praise.
We pray that you will bless
Our pledge of faithfulness
On this, our day of days.

As partners in your care,
Who in your worship share,
We bring our joy and praise.
Grant true and mutual care
As we our love declare
On this, our day of days. Amen.

99. Creator of Life

Wedding Service

10.10.11.11.
(LYONS)

LAVON BAYLER

Creator of life and Lover of all,
We gather, your gracious gifts to recall.
You bless us with families who, showing your care,
Have taught us to listen, to help, and to share.

We witness today the vows that unite
These friends who in one another delight.
We welcome their joy as a gift from your hand
And celebrate with them the love you expand.

In sadness and joy, in sickness and health,
In poverty or achievement and wealth,
We pray, gracious God, that they faithful remain
To covenant vows that true love will sustain.

Whatever their years together may hold,
We ask that your grace and promise may mold
Deep trust and forgiveness for ev'ry event
And strength in your service, wher'er they are sent. Amen.

100. In Life and Death

Funeral or Memorial Service

8.6.8.6. *(C.M.)*
(SERENITY)

LAVON BAYLER

In life and death your help is near
To comfort and to bless;
May we your reassurance hear,
O God, in our distress.

As your own child was sacrificed
To evil unrestrained,
We come to you, in Jesus Christ,
With loss we have sustained.

We celebrate the joy we knew
When life was at its best,
When all your promises seemed true
And outcomes worth the quest.

Now pain and doubts our vision cloud
And loneliness consumes.
Yet we would trust, with hearts unbowed,
The Love that empties tombs.

Grant resurrection as we grieve,
And solace in our strife.
May we your greatest gift receive,
In love: eternal life. Amen.

Indexes

Alphabetical Index of Hymns

Metrical Index of Hymns

11.10.11.10.11.10.

O Strong and Mighty God   58

11.11.11.11.

Blow Trumpets in Zion   25
Come, Sisters and Brothers   71

God Offers Forgiveness   2
We Praise You, Creator   93

Irregular

Break Forth in Singing   8

Topical Index of Hymns

ADORATION AND PRAISE

Blessed Are the Ones   75
Celebrate God's Love   95
God of All People   12
God, We Rejoice   90
God, Who Offers Life   27
God, Whose Word Brought Light   13
Grace Extends to All   54
Holy, Holy, Holy God   52
Make a Joyful Noise   48
My Heart Exults in God   87
On This, Our Day of Days   98
Praise, All Congregations   47
Praise Be to God   91
Praise God, You Mighty
   Firmament   42
Praise Our God   19
Saints, Rejoice and Sing   89
Thank You, God   40
We Give You Thanks   18
We Praise You, Creator   93

ADVENT 1–4

God Reigns, Let Earth Rejoice   7
God, Who Made This Earth   11
Rejoice, the Time Has Come   10
We Are Your People   86
We Hear Your New Song   5

ANXIETY

Amid the Storms   57
God, We Rejoice   90
Hear Us, O God   78
My God, Why?   38
O God, We Seek You   20
Steadfast Love of God   34
We Bring Our Sorrow   33
We Come, One Body   37

We Trust, O God, in You   81
Who Will Roll the Stone Away?   41

ASSURANCE

Be Still and Know   55
Christ Is Our Perfect Peace   62
God Offers Forgiveness   2
God's Rainbow Covenant   26
Make Melody to God   67
O, Sing Aloud   79
We Bring Our Sorrow   33
Who Will Roll the Stone Away?   41

BAPTISM

Glory to God   15
God, Who Offers Life   27
Make a Joyful Noise   48
Praise Be to God   91
We Cry to You, Creator   64

CHRISTMAS SEASON 5–13

We Hear Your Messenger   85

CHURCH

Celebrate God's Love   95
Christ Is Our Perfect Peace   62
Come, Christ of God   32
For the Poor   72
God, Who Blessed Us   97
Praise, All Congregations   47
Speak, O Sovereign God   16
We Come, One Body   37
We Give You Thanks   18
We Hear Your Messenger   85
We Praise You, Creator   93
Within Your Temple   31

COMFORT

All Things Are Possible 4
Blessed Are God's People 21
Break Forth in Singing 8
Creator, Be Not Angry 1
God Offers Forgiveness 2
God, Whose Word Brought Light 13
Great God, We Bring 53
Hear the Voice of God 22
In Life and Death 100
O, Sing Aloud 79
Praise Our God 19
We Cry to You, Creator 64
Who Will Roll the Stone Away? 41

COMMUNION

Come, Share the Joy 43
Make Melody to God 67
My Heart Exults in God 87
Praise Be to God 91
We Come, One Body 37
We Cry to You, Creator 64
When Christ Is Seen 49

CONFESSION

Blessed Are God's People 21
Creator, Be Not Angry 1
Deliver Us, Most Gracious God 61
For the Poor 72
God of Mystery and Grace 88
Have Mercy, God 24
Holy, Holy, Holy God 52
How Have We Despised Your
    Word? 63
How Shall We Sing? 30
My God, Why? 38
We Come, One Body 37

CONSECRATION, DEDICATION

All Things Are Possible 4
Be Still and Know 55
Faith in the Name 45
For the Poor 72
Glory to God 15
Grant Us Your Joy 50
Hear All Our Prayers 65
Ministers by God's Grace 92
Most Gracious God 96
O Strong and Mighty God 58
Rejoice, the Time Has Come 10
Speak, O Sovereign God 16

We Are Your People 86
We Come, One Body 37
We Love You, Christ 80
Within Your Temple 31
Your Word Is True, O God 60

COURAGE

Be Patient as You Wait 74
Be Still and Know 55
Creator, Be Not Angry 1
Every Gift and Good Endowment 70
Jesus Christ Is Our Good
    Shepherd 46
Lift Up Your Eyes 69
Steadfast Love of God 34
What Shall We Do, O Christ? 77

COVENANT

All Things Are Possible 4
Celebrate God's Love 95
Christ Is Our Perfect Peace 62
Creator of Life 99
Give Thanks to God 9
God of Our Parents 59
God, Who Dawns as Morning 68
God's Rainbow Covenant 26
Hear the Voice of God 22
In These Days 83
Proclaim the Glorious Splendor 82
Speak, Mighty One 23
The Works of God 28
We Come, One Body 37
We Give You Thanks 18
Within Your Temple 31
Your Word Is True, O God 60

DISCIPLESHIP

Be Still and Know 55
Blessed Are God's People 21
Come, Sisters and Brothers 71
God of Mystery and Grace 88
God of Our Parents 59
Most Gracious God 96
My God, Why? 38
O God, as We Come 66
O God, Our Refuge 35
Rejoice, God's Spirit Comes 3
Speak, Mighty One 23
Speak, O Sovereign God 16
Thank You, God 40
We Love You, Christ 80
We Praise You, Creator 93

When Christ Is Seen   49
Within Your Temple   31

DEATH

In Life and Death   100
Saints, Rejoice and Sing   89
We Bring Our Sorrow   33

DOUBT

Come, Share the Joy   43
God of Mystery and Grace   88
Make Melody to God   67
Steadfast Love of God   34
We Bring Our Sorrow   33

EASTER SEASON 39–50
EPIPHANY SEASON 14–23
ETERNAL LIFE

Be Pleased, O God   36
Come, Share the Joy   43
God of Mystery and Grace   88
God, Who Made This Earth   11
How Shall We Sing?   30
In Life and Death   100
On This Day of Expectation   51
Praise, All Congregations   47
We Trust, O God, in You   81
What Shall We Do, O Christ?   77
Where Have They Taken Christ?   39

EVANGELISM

Amid the Storms   57
Celebrate God's Love   95
Come, Sisters and Brothers   71
Faith in the Name of Jesus   45
Grace Extends to All   54
Jesus Christ Is Our Good
    Shepherd   46
O God, as We Come   66
Praise Our God   19
Proclaim the Glorious Splendor   82
Rejoice, the Day Has Come   10
We Give You Thanks   18
When Christ Is Seen   49

FAITH AND ASPIRATION

Be Still and Know   55
Creator, Be Not Angry   1
Every Gift and Good Endowment   70
Faith in the Name of Jesus   45

Glory to God   15
God of Our Parents   59
God, Who Made This Earth   11
God, Whose Word Brought Light   13
O God, We Seek You   20
O, Sing Aloud   79
Praise, All Congregations   47
Speak, O Sovereign God   16
Walking by Faith, Not Sight   56
We Cry to You, Creator   64
We Hear Your New Song   5
You Reign, O God   84

FAITHFULNESS

All Things Are Possible   4
Be Pleased, O God   36
Blessed Are the Ones   75
Come, Sisters and Brothers   71
God, Who Dawns as Morning   68
Hear the Voice of God   22
Let All Our Words   29
Lift Up Your Eyes   69
Make a Joyful Noise   48
Most Gracious God   96
My God, Why?   38
On This, Our Day of Days   98
Praise Our God   19
Rejoice, God's Spirit Comes   3
Speak, Mighty One   23
Speak, O Sovereign God   16
The Works of God   28
We Give You Thanks   18
We Trust, O God, in You   81

FORGIVENESS

Blow Trumpets in Zion   25
Creator, Be Not Angry   1
Creator of Life   99
Deliver Us, Most Gracious God   61
God of All People   12
Grace Extends to All   54
Grant Sabbath Rest   76
Have Mercy, God   24
Hear All Our Prayers   65
Hear Us, O God   78
Holy, Holy, Holy God   52
How Have We Despised Your
    Word?   63
Ministers by God's Grace   92
My God, Why?   38
O God, as We Come   66
O Strong and Mighty God   58

GOSPEL

GRACE

HEALTH AND HEALING

HOLY SPIRIT

HOLY WEEK 32–38
HOPE

JESUS CHRIST

JOY

JUSTICE

LENTEN SEASON 24–38
LIGHT

LOVE OF NEIGHBOR

MARRIAGE

MERCY

MINISTRY AND MISSION

Index of Scripture Readings

Index of Themes and Key Words

Easter Sunday
Pentecost 16
Thanksgiving Day
God's glory
Christmas Eve/Day
Epiphany 1 (Baptism of Jesus)
God's glory in Christ
Epiphany, Last Sunday
(Transfiguration)
God's goodness
Pentecost 19
God's greatness
Christmas Day (Alt. 1)
Epiphany 1 (Baptism of Jesus)
Lent 3
Pentecost 8
God's law
Lent 3
Easter 7
God's leading
Epiphany 1 (Baptism of Jesus)
Easter 4, 5
God's love
Christmas Eve/Day
Epiphany 5, 8
Lent 6 (Palm Sunday)
Easter 2, 4, 5
Trinity Sunday
God's mystery
Epiphany 1 (Baptism of Jesus)
Pentecost 15
God's power
Lent 3
Pentecost 2
Holy Cross (Sept. 14)
God's presence
Advent 4
Christmas Day (Alt. 1)
Epiphany 6
Lent 2
Lent 6 (Passion Sunday)
Pentecost 4, 7, 8, 26
God's promises
Epiphany 1 (Baptism of Jesus), 7
Lent 2
Pentecost 24
God's providence
Christmas 2
Easter 4
Pentecost 14
Holy Cross (Sept. 14)
God's purposes
Advent 4
Epiphany 1 (Baptism of Jesus), 5

God's realm
Epiphany 3
Ascension
Pentecost 4, 20
Thanksgiving Day
God's reign
Christmas Day (Alt. 1)
Christmas Day (Alt. 2)
Pentecost 25, 26, 27
God's saving acts
Lent 1, 5
Easter Sunday
Easter (Alt.)
God's Spirit
Epiphany 6
God's way(s)
Jan. 1 (Jesus & Mary)
Epiphany 3
Lent 1
Pentecost 20
God's whispers
Pentecost 17
God's will
Pentecost 7
Annunciation (Mar. 25)
All Saints (Nov. 1)
God's Word
Christmas Day (Alt. 2)
Epiphany, Last Sunday
(Transfiguration)
God's work(s)
Christmas 1
Lent 2
Good news
Advent 1, 2, 3
Christmas Eve/Day
Christmas Day (Alt. 1)
Christmas Day (Alt. 2)
Epiphany 3, 5
Easter Sunday
Easter (Alt.)
Easter Evening
Easter 2
Pentecost 17, 21
Presentation (Feb. 2)
Grace
Advent 1
Christmas Eve/Day
Christmas Day (Alt. 1)
Christmas 1, 2
Epiphany 4, 7, 8
Ash Wednesday
Easter Sunday
Pentecost 5, 7, 8, 22

Selflessness
  Pentecost 4
Servants
  Epiphany 2
  Lent 5
  Monday of Holy Week
Service
  Advent 3
  Epiphany 2, 4, 5, 7, Last Sunday
  (Transfiguration)
  Easter 6
  Pentecost 3, 6, 14, 22, 23
Shadows
  Epiphany 1 (Baptism of Jesus)
  Lent 4, 6 (Passion Sunday)
  Monday of Holy Week
  Tuesday of Holy Week
Shame
  Lent 6 (Passion Sunday)
  Monday of Holy Week
  Tuesday of Holy Week
  Wednesday of Holy Week
Sharing
  Epiphany 1 (Baptism of Jesus)
  Easter 2
  Pentecost 10, 17
Shepherd
  Easter 4
Silence
  Epiphany 3
Sin
  Wednesday of Holy Week
  Pentecost 5, 6
  Presentation (Feb. 2)
Singing
  Christmas Day (Alt. 2)
  Jan. 1 (Jesus & Mary)
  Easter 6
  Presentation (Feb. 2)
Sisters and brothers
  Annunciation (Mar. 25)
Solemnity
  Ash Wednesday
Sorrow
  Maundy Thursday
Spiritual growth
  Christmas 2
Star
  Epiphany
Steadfast love
  Advent 4
  Christmas Day (Alt. 2)
  Epiphany 5, 6, 8
  Ash Wednesday

Lent 4, 6 (Passion Sunday)
  Monday of Holy Week
  Easter 6
  Pentecost 3, 5, 7, 10, 12
  Annunciation (Mar. 25)
  Holy Cross (Sept. 14)
Steadfastness
  Pentecost 19
Stillness
  Pentecost 4
Stones
  Pentecost 12
Storms
  Pentecost 5
Strangers
  Pentecost 9
Strength
  Lent 3
  Pentecost 22
  Visitation (May 31)
  All Saints (Nov. 1)
Suffering
  Advent 2
  Lent 6 (Passion Sunday)
  Good Friday
Teaching
  Epiphany, Last Sunday
  (Transfiguration)
  Wednesday of Holy Week
  Pentecost 24
Tears
  All Saints (Nov. 1)
Temptation
  Pentecost 22
  Presentation (Feb. 2)
Tents of wickedness
  Presentation (Feb. 2)
Thankfulness
  Pentecost 14
Thanksgiving
  Christmas 2
  Pentecost 13, 23
Tithes and Offerings
  Presentation (Feb. 2)
Traditions
  Pentecost 15
Treasures in heaven
  Ash Wednesday
Trust
  Advent 4
  Epiphany 3
  Lent 6 (Passion Sunday)
  Tuesday of Holy Week
  Good Friday

About the Author

Lavon Bayler grew up in parsonages in Ohio, Indiana, and Iowa, immersed in the language of worship. As a teenager, she was active in the Youth Fellowship of the Evangelical and Reformed Church, benefiting from many of the leadership development experiences offered through workshops, national youth caravans, and denominational and ecumenical assemblies. As a youth delegate, she was instrumental in persuading the General Synod to approve plans for a denominational Voluntary Service Program. Midway through college preparations for high school teaching, she felt the call to ministry, and responded to it at a National Conference on Christian Education.

After graduation from Iowa State Teachers College and a year as national Youth Associate, Lavon (Burrichter) enrolled at Lancaster Seminary to begin preparations for an overseas missionary assignment or pastoring a local church. She met her husband, Bob Bayler, there, and the two of them completed their seminary degrees at Eden. Their first parish was a four-point charge in central Ohio, where they served as co-pastors.

Lavon Bayler spent twenty years as a local church pastor before joining the staff of the Illinois Conference in 1979. She is currently Area Conference Minister in Northern Association of the Illinois Conference, United Church of Christ, with responsibilities in placement, program planning, and resourcing of congregations. She began writing liturgical resources while serving First Congregational United Church of Christ in Carpentersville, Illinois. Early in her Conference staff career, she prepared lectionary-based resources for the clergy in her Association for their lenten usage. At their request she continued to distribute a similar gift to them every year.

Some of these resources appeared in *Bread for the Journey* and *Flames of the Spirit*. A three-month sabbatical in 1985–86 gave Pastor Bayler time to develop resources for an entire year that became her first book, *Fresh Winds of the Spirit: Liturgical Resources for Year A*. *Whispers of God: Liturgical Resources for Year B*, is the second book of a trilogy published by The Pilgrim Press.

The Baylers live in Elgin, Illinois, with their three sons, David, a proofreader and editor, who prepared indexes for both books, Jonathan, a retail manager, and Timothy, a student at Northwestern University. Bob Bayler is Vice-President for Religion and Health for the UCC's Evangelical Health Systems.